Praise for Jon Spoelstra's First Book
Ice to Eskimos

"Of the many business books published each year, those in the 'marketing advice' category lead the way in dubious value. But every now and then one comes along that actually has something to say — like Jon Spoelstra's *Ice to Eskimos* . . . Mr. Spoelstra is one of those guys who thinks 'out of the box.'"

The Wall Street Journal

"Jon Spoelstra is brilliant, brilliant, brilliant! If you're a CEO, hire him. If you want to be a CEO, read his book right away."

Al Ries
Author of *Focus*

"I've known Jon Spoelstra for many years and I consider him the top marketer in the world. In *Ice to the Eskimos,* Jon takes his secrets of sports marketing and shows how easily it works with any company. I loved it!"

Pat Williams
Founder, Orlando Magic

"This is a superb book. I couldn't put it down. I kept quoting it to everyone I ran into. Jon Spoelstra knows his stuff, and has a proven, no-baloney message for all of us."

Tom Peters
Author of *In Search of Excellence*

"There are so many fresh marketing ideas in Jon Spoelstra's book that it will jump-start any company whether it be a two-person lemonade stand or mega corporation."

Harvey Mackay
Author of *Swim with the Sharks Without Being Eaten Alive*

"Jon Spoelstra is the Doctor J of sports marketing, a man who actually got people to buy New Jersey Nets tickets. In this book, he gives a marketing clinic and puts on his most dazzling moves."

John Helyar
Coauthor of *Barbarians at the Gate*

"In today's marketplace, it is critical to have a solid game plan off the court so you can control the bottom line even when there are other elements that go beyond your control on the court. Jon Spoelstra's book lays out that game plan for you step-by-step."

Pat Riley
President, Miami Heat

"Jon Spoelstra has a very creative marketing mind. Everyone can learn something from reading his book."

Philip H. Knight
Chairman and CEO, Nike

PRAISE FOR *MARKETING OUTRAGEOUSLY*

"Spoelstra offers an amazing array of examples, suggestions, tips, and steps toward increasing revenue through unconventional means. *Marketing Outrageously* provides numerous entertaining anecdotes about his marketing genius, and serves as a guide from which any salesperson or marketing executive could glean the skills to push the marketing envelope."

Executive Book Summaries

"Spoelstra offers another fine book on creative marketing strategies and motivation . . . is instructive in its marketing ideas and stories of triumph . . . will be useful to professional marketers and students of marketing."

Library Journal

"This book shows you how to jump-start your revenue so you can work your way out of a slumping economy . . . gives 17 ground rules that help to raise top and bottom lines."

Sales & Marketing Strategies and News

"Spoelstra's philosophy has served him well. By using unorthodox resources, he has helped profits of several professional teams skyrocket."

Continental Airlines magazine

"You can be *The Titanic* (the movie) with Spoelstra's outrageous marketing strategies, or you can be the *Titanic* (the boat) if your competitor takes these ideas and runs with them. Be the movie."

Peter Guber
Chairman
Mandalay Entertainment

"This is a one-in-a-million book that will make a profound difference in your company's revenue growth. Jon Spoelstra has woven a collection of ingenious marketing tactics in an entertaining and inspiring way."

Masato Mizuno
President
Mizuno Corporation

"I really, really, really enjoyed the book! It's a great read, and it gave me instantly actionable advice. In a world full of marketing clutter, it gets to the real root of marketing success and lays out a map for change today. I have new inspiration on how to use 'rubber chickens.'"

Greg J. Peterson
Partner–Transaction Services
PricewaterhouseCoopers LLP

"In today's markets, you have to market outrageously! That's precisely what Jon Spoelstra shows you how to do in his latest explosive and entertaining handbook. You'd better read *Marketing Outrageously* before your competitors do, so you won't have to pay the big price for marketing ignorance — lower revenue."

Frank Perez
President & CEO
Kettering Medical Center Network

"Learn the counterintuitive techniques of *Marketing Outrageously* and watch your profits soar. Opportunity and security rarely come in the same package. No one knows this better than Jon Spoelstra."

Roy H. Williams
Author of *The Wizard of Ads* and the *New York Times* bestseller *Secret Formulas of the Wizard of Ads*

"Jon Spoelstra and his advice are world class. This is a MUST OWN, MUST READ, and MUST IMPLEMENT book on real-world marketing ideas and strategies you can apply to your business right now . . . and turn them into money."

Jeffrey Gitomer
Author of *The Little Red Book of Selling* and
The Little Black Book of Connections

"*Marketing Outrageously* could be titled '*Marketing Intelligently*,' or '*Marketing Sensibly*,' because any marketing that does not follow Jon's principles is really the outrageous kind of marketing. His principles are brilliant, realistic, and perfect for a new century when it is tougher than ever to stand out from the marketing hordes. Here's a high five to Jon and a powerful recommendation for anyone in any kind of business to read and take each word to heart."

Jay Conrad Levinson
Author of the *Guerrilla Marketing* series of books

"If you want to get your employees committed to a new, positive, supercharged way of thinking about revenue, here's the book that will do it. It's full of ideas that will challenge their thinking and motivate them to action."

Joe Sugarman
Chairman
BluBlocker Sunglasses

Books by Jon Spoelstra

Non-Fiction

*Marketing Outrageously Redux: How to Increase Your Revenue
   by Staggering Amounts*
   Bard Press, Austin 2010

*Marketing Outrageously: How to Increase Your Revenue by
   Staggering Amounts*
   Bard Press, Austin 2001

Ice to the Eskimos: How to Market a Product Nobody Wants
   Harper Business, New York 1997

Success Is Just One Wish Away
   Delstar, Las Vegas 1999

Your Profits Are Brought to You by....
   SRO Partners, 1991; available at jonspoelstra.com

How to Sell the Last Seat in the House
   SRO Partners, 1990; available at jonspoelstra.com

Fiction

*Red Chaser: A Noir Thriller of the 1950s, the Cold War,
   and the Brooklyn Dodgers*
   Electronic Edition 2008

MARKETING
OUTRAGEOUSLY
REDUX
Revised Edition

How to Increase Your Revenue
by Staggering Amounts!

JON SPOELSTRA
FOREWORD BY MARK CUBAN

Austin, Texas

MARKETING OUTRAGEOUSLY REDUX
Revised Edition
How to Increase Your Revenue by Staggering Amounts!
Jon Spoelstra

Copyright © 2010 by Jon Spoelstra
All rights reserved
Printed in USA

Permission to reproduce or transmit in any form or by any means, electronic or mechanical, including photocopying and recording, or by an information storage and retrieval system, must be obtained by contacting

Bard Press
5275 McCormick Mtn Dr
Austin, Texas 78734

512-266-2112 phone, 512-266-2749 fax
info@bardpress.com
Visit our website: www.bardpress.com

ORDERING INFORMATION
To order additional copies, contact your local bookstore or
e-mail info@bardpress.com. Quantity discounts are available.

ISBN 13-digit 978-1-885167-73-6, 10-digit 1-885167-73-3   Paperback

Library of Congress Cataloging-in-Publication Data
Spoelstra, Jon.

      Marketing outrageously redux : how to increase your revenue by staggering amounts! / Jon Spoelstra foreword by Mark Cuban. -- Rev. ed.
         p. cm.
      Rev. ed. of: Marketing outrageously : how to increase your revenue by staggering amounts! 2001.

    Includes bibliographical references and index.
    ISBN 978-1-885167-73-6 (alk. paper)
   1. Marketing. I. Spoelstra, Jon. Marketing outrageously. II. Title.

   HF5415.S726 2010
   658.8--dc22   2010040734

The author may be contacted at the following address:
   Jon Spoelstra
   7700 SW Northvale
   Portland, OR 97225

503-706-6601 phone
findjon@msn.com e-mail

CREDITS

First Edition
Editing: Jeff Morris
Proofreading: Deborah
   Costenbader, Luke Torn
Text Design/Production:
   Hespenheide Design
Jacket Design: Hespenheide Design
Cover Photograph: Scott Hirko
Cover Model: Big Nate, Coralie Jr.
   Theatrical Agency
Index: Alana Cash

Revised Edition
Managing Editor: Sherry Sprague
Copyeditor/Production Editor: Deborah
   Costenbader
Proofreading: Deborah Costenbader,
   Luke Torn
Jacket Design: Hespenheide Design
Cover Photograph: Scott Hirko
Cover Model: Big Nate, Coralie Jr.
   Theatrical Agency
Index: Linda Webster

First Edition Hardcover
First printing: June 2001
Second printing: July 2001
Third printing: August 2002
Fourth printing: April 2003
Fifth printing: October 2004
Sixth printing: December 2005
Seventh printing: July 2008
Eighth printing: October 2009

First Edition Paperback
First printing: December 2010

TABLE OF CONTENTS

Why Didn't I Think of That?

Jon Spoelstra did. His stuff is intuitive, not complicated, cuts right to the nub, and most of all, it works so easily that folks wonder why they didn't think of that solution.

Jon's focus is on measurable results that impact the bottom line — without big marketing or big advertising budgets. Going beyond marketing "theory," his approach encourages pushing the outrageous envelope to differentiate a service or product and gain immediate sales.

He has been called "the top marketer in the world." Jon's outrageous methods, such as the Rubber Chicken, are legendary. Most of his life he has run pro sports teams, as the general manager of the NBA's Portland Trail Blazers and then as president of the New Jersey Nets. His next stop was president of the Mandalay Baseball Properties, where he built a group of seven minor-league baseball teams into a thriving enterprise.

His marketing campaigns have sold out stadiums for record runs and boosted revenue and profit by amazing amounts.

Jon has consulted with many companies, including sports organizations in the United States, Spain, and Japan. He has been a college professor and is the author of seven books. He is now a writer, speaker, and consultant.

To reach Jon with your comments or to make arrangements for him to speak at your next meeting, contact him at findjon@msn.com.

Foreword

If you're a pro basketball fan, you can probably guess why I'm writing the foreword to *Marketing Outrageously*. Since buying the Dallas Mavericks in January 2000, I've done some outrageous things, from providing limos to take our players to our games to giving free tickets to fans who come to road games painted in Mavs colors. I've tried to take the Dallas Mavericks, and our marketing, not only to our fans and customers but to our players and the entire NBA as well.

Some considered it outrageous when I gave out my e-mail address on national TV and radio, and at every game, and *personally* answered each response. To me, they were customers saying they were interested in my team. Would you not return a prospect's or customer's phone call? Was it outrageous when I asked every fan to join me in the owner's box, which for me happens to be the seats at the very top of our arena? Some people thought so. Those seats started selling out three games later.

I provided plush towels with the Mavericks logo to all of our players. After all, who wants to dry off from a shower in a raggedy towel? Some people thought I was outrageous when I gave them not only to my players but to all the visiting players as well. To me it was a way to send a message to potential free agents who might want to play for the Mavs that we're a first-class organization that treats them better than their current team. The towels cost under $10 each, and yes, the visiting players *always* take them

Mark Cuban
Cofounder, Broadcast.com;
Owner, Dallas Mavericks

home with them! I also provide the visiting players with a complete buffet after every game, something no other team in the NBA does. All the players notice and talk about it. A little bit of outrageous marketing can mean my getting the best possible employees and, in turn, giving my customers the best possible experiences!

If you're familiar with the dot.com world, you'll know me from my years when I cofounded Broadcast.com, when I was outrageous enough to believe that sports fans would take $3,000 and $4,000 computers and connect them to the Internet to make them work like $5 transistor radios so they could listen to their favorite sports teams over the net from around the world. From the second bedroom of my house, my partner Todd Wagner and I turned Broadcast.com into a business that we sold to Yahoo in 1999 for more than $5.7 *billion.*

To me none of this is outrageous. It's common sense. But thank goodness so few others think like Jon Spoelstra and me.

I learned about Jon Spoelstra's outrageous thinking in his first book, *Ice to the Eskimos.* When I bought the Mavericks, I was looking for a kindred soul with new ideas I could steal. And Jon has them. I've become a big fan. Other Mavs staffers and I regularly e-mail Jon to get his reaction to our ideas. So when he asked me to write the foreword to *Marketing Outrageously,* I was more than happy to comply.

In the sports world, Jon is a legend. His record of dramatically increasing revenue at the Portland Trail Blazers and New Jersey Nets is remarkable. His two workbooks, *How to Sell the Last Seat in the House* and *Your Profits Are Brought to You by Sponsorships,* sold a ton directly into the sports market, even at the outrageous prices of $800 and $1,600 each.

Jon's new book is a terrific guide on how to think and act if you want to turbocharge your sales. In the first chapter he explains that marketing outrageously is the only way to really grow your company — that it's far more dangerous to market conservatively. I totally agree. My experience in the dot.com world, as well as the sports world, strongly supports Jon's contention. Don't let the sports stories mislead you into thinking that these ideas apply only to sports. There are lots of examples like Aflac, Hyundai, and Vidalia Onion that demonstrate that these ideas work in all companies.

This book is packed with provocative ideas, like how to use a rubber chicken to get people's attention and how to attract new customers by giving your products or services away. It's a real nuts-and-bolts book, too. It will challenge you and other people in your company. Jon's title question in chapter 2, "What's It Gonna Take?" will get you thinking about how you set goals. In chapter 15 he has yet another big, but practical, question that everyone in your company should be asking: "What Have I Done to Make Money for My Company Today?"

It's not often that I find myself continuously referring to a book for motivation and guidance. But that's exactly what I do with *Marketing Outrageously*. It's the ultimate guide for taking companies of any size to a new level. It's full of crazy, fun ideas that can help anyone sell more. In fact, I found myself trying to out-outrageous Jon's ideas. *Marketing Outrageously* is the cure for "marketer's block." You can't help pushing the envelope after reading it.

I highly recommend this book. It will be required reading for every Dallas Maverick employee and a gift to many of my friends.

Mark Cuban
Owner, Dallas Mavericks

I Shoulda Bought a Rubber Chicken Factory

S ince *Marketing Outrageously* was first published in 2001, I've received over 4,000 e-mails from readers. (My personal e-mail address, by the way, is findjon@msn.com.)

I answered each e-mail. One of the most popular topics of the e-mails was: "Where can I buy rubber chickens?" (You'll have to read how I used rubber chickens in chapter 12.)

I gave my readers a place where they could buy them. Now, of course, you can easily find where to buy rubber chickens on the Internet. In fact, Amazon.com offers them for less than three bucks each!

Over the years, I got e-mails explaining how some of my readers used rubber chickens.

> A real estate broker used rubber chickens.
> A banker!
> A trucking company.
> Insurance agency, of course.
> A car dealer.
> A nursery of plants and trees.
> A paving company.
> A construction company.
> And, a cemetery!

Each of these companies used the rubber chicken in a very clever (and different) manner in grabbing somebody's attention.

Some told me that they ordered 25 rubber chickens to grab attention. Others bought over 100 rubber chickens. One ordered over 500. It got me to thinking: I shoulda bought a rubber chicken factory! It also got me thinking that market-ing ideas are easily transferable to different industries — from a banker to a nursery to a cemetery!

That's why I have written *Marketing Outrageously Redux*. The ideas in the original *Marketing Outrageously* have now been time-tested for another ten years. In *Marketing Outrageously Redux*, I've updated those ideas with plenty of new examples of how a seemingly outrageous idea can actu-ally produce real live outrageous results for you.

When you're reading *Marketing Outrageously Redux*, you'll feel this strong urge to adapt many of the ideas to your business. So, get a pen and a pad of paper ready, and as you read jot down ideas that will help you raise revenue in stag-gering amounts.

Jon Spoelstra
September 2010

CHAPTER 1

Do You Have the Guts?

Right off the bat, I'm asking you to do something.

It's easy. Look at the years listed below. I want you to circle one of those years. Pick the year that was important to you: it could be the year you got married, or got a new job, or started a company. Something important. Go ahead and circle it.

1969	1982
1970	1990
1973	1991
1974	2001
1975	2007
1980	2008
1981	2009

Now I'd like you to repeat the exercise. Circle another year that was important to you. Go ahead, mark up the book with another circle.

Those years listed are the years that the U.S. federal government designated as official recession years. Those are the hard times. Those are the times that get men and women to shake in their boots. But, take a look. You've circled two of those years as important milestone years for you.

Greatest Successes in a Bad Economy

When I first wrote *Marketing Outrageously,* I realized that my greatest successes were in a crummy economy. That made me pause. Why were my greatest personal successes in a bad economy? That wasn't logical. I looked at my performance in the years with a good economy. I wasn't lousy; in fact, I did well. After thinking it through, I realized that it was more difficult to distinguish myself in a great economy. Heck, even the dummies did well in a great economy. It was a rotten economy that provided the *best opportunity to shine.*

Sure, I had some terrific successes in a good economy, but I had outrageous successes when the economy was deemed awful by the federal government. So, I came to a simple conclusion: always (always, always) market your product as if it is a lousy economy. In other words, always (that's right, always) market outrageously. After all, if it works in a bad economy, why in all Billy Hell wouldn't you market outrageously in a good economy?

What's Outrageous About Outrageous?

You may now be wondering, "What does he mean by outrageous? And why would any responsible businessperson want to market outrageously?" It's a good question, and one that deserves a thoughtful and detailed answer. That's why I'm writing this book.

For the long answer, you need to read the whole book. This will give you plenty of good examples of outrageous marketing and the reasons it works, along with some useful pointers and guidelines about how to do it. And as you read and enjoy the book, you'll find at the end of each chapter some questions that will remind you of what you're learning. They are easy questions. They are no-brainer questions. They're outrageous questions. You can look up most of the answers in the book. Some of the answers, however, aren't in the book. You have to come up with them by applying the principles of Marketing Outrageously to your own business. You can skip them and go to the next chapter if you prefer. But if you read them and think about them, you'll learn more about Marketing Outrageously.

Okay, for you impatient types who want an easy, if incomplete, short answer, I'll give you several. Each is a partial answer that tells you something about Marketing Outrageously without giving away the whole thing — the way the seven legendary blind men described the elephant.

- Marketing Outrageously is fun.

- Marketing Outrageously is politically incorrect.

- Marketing Outrageously is using your imagination.

- Marketing Outrageously is being willing to be laughed at.

- Marketing Outrageously is putting revenue first and everything else second.

- Marketing Outrageously is dropping your assumptions and starting over with a fresh point of view.

- Marketing Outrageously is the opposite of marketing safely — but it may be the only truly safe way to market.

Okay, I can hear you. You're still asking, "What does he mean, 'Marketing Outrageously'?" It's time for another example.

What Desperate Men Do

Their backs were clearly against the wall, and desperate times called for desperate measures. In this case, their desperate measure was summoning me.

"They" were the seven owners of the New Jersey Nets — the Secaucus Seven, as the local newspapers called them, as in the Seven Dwarfs, not the Magnificent Seven. These guys had owned the Nets for fourteen years, during which the team had been consistently lousy. They usually broke even, but they could never make any real money.

Being able to break even was due mainly to NBA economics. Since 1983, there had been a cap on team salaries. With fixed expenses thus limited, the teams that prospered were those that generated the most revenue. Some teams wisely spent their limit on great players who drew fans to the arenas. Others, like the Nets, put their money into underachievers and malcontents.

In the early 1990s, the Nets were more dismal than ever. Player contracts were skyrocketing, but the Nets still couldn't get people to come to their games. Now the Nets could be really awful and lose a lot of money in the process — $4 to $5 million a season. Even if you're very rich, losing that kind of money isn't much fun.

The owners tried deeply discounting thousands and thousands of tickets. It didn't work. They tried giving away tens of thousands of tickets. The more they gave away, the more people stopped buying tickets, even discounted tickets.

"Look at this," one owner said. He handed me an empty milk carton. On the side was an offer: "Milk the Nets for $4." For just $4, you could buy a $20 ticket to see a game against Michael Jordan and the Chicago Bulls or the Nets' cross-river rivals, the New York Knicks.

"They used to have a picture of missing kids. The milk company told us they found more missing kids than we sold tickets.

"We've tried everything, and we've failed. We can't move the team because of our lease with the arena. There would be huge penalties. We need your ideas on how to get people to go to our games."

An Outrageous Plan

Even though the Nets were lousy, I felt we could boost their revenue with some unconventional marketing. I wrote a seventy-page marketing recommendation and sent a copy to each owner.

Here are the high points:

1. **Ignore Manhattan.** We would ignore the siren call of nearby Manhattan, where basketball fans cheered for the Knicks or nobody, and market to northern New Jersey, the eighth largest market in the United States.

2. **Market the other guys.** We would market the Nets on the backs of their opponents. Instead of trying to drum up hometown loyalty for a lousy team, we would publicize appearances of our opponents' superstars, like Michael Jordan, Shaquille O'Neal, Charles Barkley, and Patrick Ewing.

3. **Families were our niche.** We would market not our players, who were mediocre at best, nor our game, which was forgettable, but family entertainment. We would make attending a Nets game an event to remember and talk about and look forward to, whether the team won or not.

A week after I mailed out my plan, we met in New Jersey. Here's the first thing one owner said:

"When I read your marketing recommendation, I got furious. In fact, I had to walk around the block two times just to cool down. Everything you recommended went against what I believed in. After I walked around the block a few more times, I started to think that this was absolutely brilliant. But I also thought it was totally outrageous. This is really Marketing Outrageously."

That's not the first time I had heard that term applied to my marketing concepts. In fact, I had gotten used to it. If I didn't hear it, I would begin to suspect something was wrong.

I told the owners, "It may sound outrageous, but it isn't. It's just unusual. But it'll work — if you have the guts."

"We've got the guts," the owner said, puffing out his chest. "But what if these ideas don't work?"

"Sell the team," I said.

I wasn't trying to be glib. It was just that if these ideas didn't work, nothing would. Fortunately, there were always people who wanted to buy NBA teams, even miserable ones.

Cut to the chase: The concepts worked. Gloriously so. In three seasons, the revenue from paid tickets went up from $5 million to $17 million. Local sponsorships ballooned from $400,000 to $7 million. Most important for the Secaucus Seven, the market value of the team grew from $40 million to more than $120 million. Two years after I left the team, they sold it for a reported $140 million.

My Most Outrageous Weakness

Let's jump ahead a few more years to another NBA team I consulted for.

"All you care about is increasing revenue," the president of that team said to me.

I nodded.

"You don't care about the ramifications that has on other departments, like the box office. The box office people are now way overworked."

I nodded again, smiling.

"You don't care that our pay scale gets all out of whack. The marketing people and salespeople are making more and more."

Again I nodded.

"That's a weakness," he said. "You're too one-dimensional, too focused on increasing revenue."

I agreed. To this president, who ran a hapless pro sports team, he was right. To the owners who brought me in, however, being so focused on revenue was a tremendous strength.

I've got a simplistic way of looking at success in business. I believe all major corporate problems stem from inadequate revenue. I've never seen a company in trouble from having too much revenue.

This book is about what I do best — increasing revenue by marketing.

What's So Outrageous About Marketing?

Corporations often try to make up for a lack of revenue by means other than marketing. Here are three trendy ways:

1. **The Investment Way and the Borrow It Way.** Somewhere along the way, the words "revenue" and "investment" and "loan" somehow came to mean the same thing. Need

cash? You can raise revenue, or you can raise investment dollars, or just borrow it. Investment is cool, because you can live in Oz. You can float wild promises and predictions and rake in millions on the stock market. Sooner or later, of course, the company will indeed have to *raise revenue and make a profit*—but that's for somebody else to worry about. You long ago cashed in on your stock options and drove away in your new Maserati.

2. **The Edward Scissorhands Approach.** Even in the best of times, companies should always be undergoing minor liposuction. Unfortunately, some companies look to a present-day Edward Scissorhands, the movie character that had multiple snapping scissors as hands, as the cost-cutting role model for increasing profits in the short term. These companies even go further; they crank up the chainsaws and cut away some fat, along with a lot of muscle and gizzard and bone. Wall Street loves this approach. The more blood on the floor, the better.

3. **Let's Make a Deal.** This is a popular solution with larger corporations. Instead of increasing revenue by marketing, it's far easier just to merge with or buy somebody. With a couple of signatures, the CEO can make it look like he doubled revenue in a blink. (Let's see you do that, marketers!) A merger looks terrific to the Wall Street folks, and it usually brings the CEO enormous bonuses.

Such bonuses should be considered blood money. The merger is usually paid with the salaries of the thousands of employees who are laid off. The merged company is "reengineered," and the new mantra is "synergy."

Synergy, by the way, doesn't work in growing the new company's revenues through marketing. "Synergy" is just a word used to justify increasing revenue by acquisition, a smoke-and-mirrors solution for the CEO who wants to head straight to his bank. Instead of "synergy," think "parachute" — as in "golden parachute" — for the CEO and a handful of other top executives.

Let's say a company does all three of these things to increase profit. What will it have to do next? Eventually, the company will have to raise revenue by marketing.

That's what this book is about: raising revenue by marketing. It sounds a bit old-fashioned — and it is, because it deals with marketing fundamentals. But to raise revenue in staggering amounts, which is the aim of Marketing Outrageously, you have to twist and pull and stretch those fundamentals. You have to push the envelope.

Raising your revenue a little bit each year is like taking steps backwards.

When you twist and pull and stretch marketing fundamentals, you're entering the world of Marketing Outrageously.

IS OUTRAGEOUS DANGEROUS?

You might say, "I'm sort of a conservative person. Outrageous sounds dangerous to me. Can I get fired doing this stuff?"

I would say to you, "It depends."

"It depends? Depends on what?"

"How big is your company?" I would ask.

If the company you work for is a mega-corporation, then Marketing Outrageously might be hazardous to your immediate health. You see, the outrageous ideas and strategies in this book are not, by themselves, dangerous. However, they are different, and in a mega-corporation, just being *different* can be risky. An outrageous marketing idea presented in writing might be considered a professional suicide note. It's far safer for your job security to do plain-vanilla marketing.

No staggering increases in revenues for you; play for a safe, steady 5 percent.

Unfortunately, the man with the hood and the tall axe will eventually come for you. He'll direct you to stretch out your neck. "Sorry," he'll say, " 5 percent increases aren't good enough. One of your competitors is using outrageous marketing and taking huge bites out of your market share." So, if you work for a mega-corporation, you might as well market outrageously. It may seem scary at first, but it's not as scary as that character with the axe. After you get over the initial shock, you'll learn safe ways to use the principles of Marketing Outrageously. And you'll look like a genius.

For a smaller company, outrageous isn't dangerous at all — in fact, *it's far more perilous to market conservatively.* To conserve means to save — as in saving yourself to become a late-night snack for a bigger, revenue-hungry competitor.

Outraging the Naysayer

I've marketed in great economic times. I've also marketed in awful economic times, with unemployment and inflation soaring. I've marketed in the Rust Belt when it seemed that every business was moving south (will the last company leaving town please turn out the lights?). There are two things that are consistent about marketing, whether in the Golden Age or the Toilet Age:

1. **Naysayers live here.** It doesn't matter what the economy is doing. Naysayers are always there, like flies in China.

A friend of my daughter spent some time in China. When he got back, we were on our deck discussing his experiences. I asked him what one image stuck in his mind. I was thinking about the Great Wall or the Forbidden City or something like that. He said, "The flies."

"The flies?" I asked.

"Flies," he said. "They're *everywhere.*"

"That can't be," I said. "I read that during the Cultural Revolution Mao asked every man, woman, and child to catch 100 flies. They wanted to eradicate flies from their country. There were a billion people living in China at that time. If each man, woman, and child did indeed catch 100 flies, then there would have been one hundred billion flies caught and killed!"

"Well," my daughter's friend said, "Maybe there were 100 billion flies hiding somewhere. Now they're out of hiding. They're everywhere!"

Naysayers and flies always survive. As China found out with flies, you can't get rid of them. Same with naysayers.

If it's a lousy economy, the naysayer will say, "We can't do that marketing outrageous stuff. We've got to be conservative. We've got to be careful."

When the biggest bull is running around in the economy, the naysayer will say, "We don't need to do that marketing outrageous stuff. We can afford to be conservative. We can afford to be careful."

These naysayers — regardless of a good or bad economy — want to label Marketing Outrageously as reckless and foolish. It's not. As I have said, it's just different. When have you found a naysayer who liked something different?

So, if you choose to employ the principles of Marketing Outrageously, prepare yourself for the naysayer. He'll be there, no doubt about it. That, by itself, isn't so bad or even dangerous. In fact, as we'll see later, having naysayers can be an advantage.

2. **Marketing Outrageously works marvelously.** You would think that Marketing Outrageously would work better in a bullish economy. Not so. Marketing Outrageously works equally well whether the economy is sluggish or booming. In this book, I'll give you examples of both.

I'll use examples from the world of sports, of course, because that's my world and the bulk of my experience. I think you'll find them entertaining, whether you're a sports fan or not — although you should be especially thankful I didn't come from the world of portable toilet sales. But I'll also provide examples of businesses large and small that have nothing to do with sports — unless cutthroat competition is your game of choice.

The Beginning and End of Each Chapter

At the beginning of each chapter, I tell a little anecdote from my experiences in the NBA and other sports, or sometimes just a story about something unusual that's happened to me. This is just my way of easing you into the chapter — my "slippery slide" (more on this later).

But once you've read it, don't stop. Keep reading. Dig into the real meat of Marketing Outrageously, because I have a little test waiting for you at the end of each chapter. In fact, here's the first test:

AN OUTRAGEOUS TEST

To help you in adapting these principles to your company, I throw in "A Simple Test You Can Take" at the end of each chapter. There's an easy way to grade this test. You don't send in your answers for a grade. If you answer the questions, you get an "A." If you just skip over the test, you don't just flunk the test, you flunk the book. So do me and yourself a favor. Just take the test and let the ideas flow.

Answer the following multiple-choice question:

1. I want to
   a. Increase the revenue of my company dramatically.
   b. Steal market share from the leaders in my field.
   c. Increase my own compensation.
   d. Increase the compensation of all the good marketing and salespeople in my company.
   e. All of the above.
   f. None of the above.
   g. Use this information to help downsize my company.

Answers

1. If you answered "e," you did terrific! You scored 150 out of a possible 100. Better yet, you'll enjoy this book and learn to apply principles of Marketing Outrageously. When you do, you'll see that they work. Your company will grow. You'll be a hero, you'll be paid a king's ransom, and your employees will consider you a saint.

If your answer was "f," I'm not sure why you've read this far. I'll award you an "incomplete." If you manage to finish the book, come back and take this test again.

If you answered "g," turn in your test and walk out the door. You must be a financial type who will be trying to learn the principles of Marketing Outrageously so that you can be a little knowledgeable when you try to kill company growth. Well, reading this book won't work for you. The book will just confirm your belief that all marketing people are crazy.

CHAPTER 2

What's It Gonna Take?

We don't set out to produce lousy movies," Peter Guber told me. Peter is the former chairman of Sony Pictures and now chairman of Mandalay Entertainment. Peter has so many Oscars and Emmys and other awards that he's run out of wall space to display them.

"The producer and director and writer don't start out thinking they're going to create a lousy movie," Peter said. "The actors certainly don't, either. After all, a real bomb could set their careers back. It sometimes just happens that even truly talented people make a bomb. For whatever reason, the chemistry just doesn't work. Then there are other times when the chemistry works perfectly, even with a small budget, and everything is wonderful and profitable."

That got me thinking of my line of work. There's not a pro sports team owner I know of who starts out with the thought of creating a lousy team, no general manager who sets out to get ripped in the media or booed by the fans. Yet many of them have turned out some unbelievably lousy teams. Imagine how lousy they could have been if they had planned it.

There are thirty teams in the National Basketball Association. Of these thirty, only four or five, at the most, are thinking during the off-season about winning the championship. These four or five teams ask themselves, "What's it going to take to win it all this year?"

Pat Riley, president of the Miami Heat, thinks championship. If the Heat goes to the NBA finals and gets beat, Riley considers the season unsuccessful. It's win the championship or nothing. There's no question that was what he was thinking when he maneuvered to get superstars LeBron James and Chris Bosh to join Heat superstar Dwyane Wade. There are a handful of teams that think the same way. Other team executives and coaches think about improving their record a bit or advancing one more round in the playoffs.

Hooray for those who think, plot, and dream to win it all *this* year.

The Question

Do you know anyone who starts out with the thought of creating a lousy company?

Don't spend much time thinking about that — you won't think of any. Sure, you know some lousy companies, but nobody started out with the concept of creating them that way.

I don't have any easy solution for those movie producers about not producing lousy movies, or the pro sports team owner on how not to produce a loser, or the businessperson on how not to create a lousy company. But I do have one suggestion.

Learn to ask this question: "What's it going to take?"

Most businesspeople are thinking, "How can we make our budget numbers?" or "How can we improve our profit over last year?" They are asking the wrong question.

What if you asked the following question at your company: "What's it going to take to be the best company in our industry *this year?*"

You don't have to be a CEO or a business owner to ask this kind of question. You could ask, "What's it going to take to become the best marketing department in the industry *this year?*" or "What's it going to take to be the best department in our company *this year?*"

I know how difficult it is to answer that question. I've asked it many times. Sometimes I've just asked myself, because it can seem too outrageous to ask anyone else. Sometimes I've asked others, even though if they'd been carrying guns I'd probably be dead. But you have to ask it, because that's the only way to come up with truly outrageous marketing ideas.

I'll give you an example. In the late 1980s, I was general manager of the Portland Trail Blazers. Even though I didn't

have the authority to draft or trade players, I could call meetings with those who did. I assembled the coaches and player personnel managers and asked the question, "What's it gonna take to win the championship this year?"

Logically, it was a foolish question. This was the era when Magic Johnson and Kareem Abdul-Jabbar were leading the Los Angeles Lakers to regular championships. When the Lakers didn't win, Larry Bird and the Boston Celtics did.

Lining up to cut in on the Lakers and Celtics were Michael Jordan and the Chicago Bulls. So how stupid was my question, "What's it going to take to win the NBA championship *this year?*"

On paper, we didn't have a chance; in our minds, less than no chance. We were, however, a pretty good team. We had won fifty-three games the year before. Considering all this, I wanted us to *think* beyond what we had.

The player personnel people took the question as an insult. I could hear them thinking, "Who does this marketing guy think he is?" They fumed and grumbled for a while.

I asked the question again. "What's it going to take to win a championship this year?"

Silence. Finally, John Wetzel, an assistant coach, said, "One thing we need to do is really improve our outside shooting. We need some guy that can come off the bench and really fill it up."

"*Two* shooters," said Rick Adelman, another assistant. "When we get to the playoffs, we can't run our fast break as much, and the middle gets clogged up. We need *two* reliable shooters coming off the bench."

We talked for two hours. Head Coach Mike Shuler was enthusiastic, salivating over the thought of somehow acquiring two bona fide outside shooters. We made a list of players who might be available. We came away from the meeting with assignments for each of us to start making inquiries with other teams.

Later, Rick Adelman told me, "I've been in a lot of player personnel meetings over the years, and this was the best. We actually talked about winning a championship and what that would take."

Did I think we had a chance to win the championship that year? Not really. But I knew we had no chance to improve unless we set the target higher than what was comfortable.

Beyond the Question

Seven years later, as president of the New Jersey Nets, I found myself asking the same question. I had no voice in choosing the players — my expertise is raising revenue in staggering amounts to pay for these guys — but I thought I'd ask anyway.

At the time, the Nets were a hapless team with a hapless past and a hapless future. The team had won only thirty games the year before and lost fifty-two. So picture the reaction from Willis Reed, our general manager, when I asked, "What's it going to take to win a championship this year?"

Willis just stared at me. The fact that Willis is one of the five nicest men I've ever met probably saved me from having my head torn off. He probably wondered if I was on drugs or was just naturally crazy.

Finally, Willis said, "Sign Michael Jordan and Karl Malone and Shaquille O'Neal as free agents."

That answer, of course, was just as crazy as my question. But I persisted: "Really, what's it going to take to win the championship this year?"

"It's not possible," Willis said.

"I can accept that," I said. I knew our cast of characters. They had multiple-year contracts. Not even the master magician David Copperfield could have made them disappear in just a year. "Let me rephrase my question. What's it going to take to win the championship *next* year?"

There was some method to these crazy questions. Most player personnel people aim to improve a little bit each year.

That's also the way most marketing managers think. Steady progress is good enough, they say.

Bunk, I say.

A team can always come up with legitimate-sounding reasons why it can't compete for a championship. Willis had one: "We don't have the money to make it next year, or the year after that, or the year after that."

Money, the Easy Scapegoat

Does this sound familiar? "We don't have the budget to be the best." Or "We don't have the budget to dramatically improve our market share." Or "We don't have the money to increase our revenue by staggering amounts."

Money. The reason for not competing for the championship or becoming the best company in the industry is always related to money. It's never "We don't think big enough." It's never "We don't have enough moxie." It's never "We don't have good enough ideas."

When I ask businesspeople the "What's it gonna take?" question and get the money answer, I always ask, "How much money would you need to become the best?" The answer is usually a little vague.

They've never really thought about it; they're usually focused on making their budget goals or improving a little bit. But they're also a little afraid. What if they did have enough money to become the best, and they still didn't make it? It's safer to be mediocre.

When Pigs Learn to Fly

Becoming the best takes more than money; it takes thinking big from the start. When lack of money pops up, then it's time for some creative thinking. That's what Marketing Outrageously is all about — modest marketing budgets, big impact.

When Willis told me that money was the reason we couldn't compete for the NBA championship, I asked my stock question, "How much is it going to take?" Now that was a legitimate question. After all, that's what I did for a

living — raise a team's revenues and profits.

Willis gave me an answer. It was more than just higher player salaries. It was a bigger scouting budget. It was a fancier private jet the team could use to travel to road games. It was a lot of things, adding up to $5 million over budget.

The $5 million was a stretch for us, I told Willis, but if that's what it took, we'd get the money. "Now," I said, "what's it gonna take to win a championship next year?"

"Well, we'll need two superstars," Willis said. "Chicago has Michael Jordan and Scottie Pippen, the Lakers have Magic and Abdul-Jabbar, the Celtics have Bird and McHale. We've got just one — Derrick Coleman — and he won't practice with the team."

Derrick Coleman was a very talented basketball player — six-foot-ten, 258 pounds of pure athlete. Unfortunately, he didn't like to compete and wouldn't practice. He didn't like basketball.

"Can we count Derrick as one of those superstars?" I asked. "There's no question about his talent, but does he have the character, the work ethic, the personality?"

"Maybe as he matures he'll develop those," Willis said.

"Let's go back to my original question. What's it going to take to win a championship next year? Do we have to wait and see if Derrick grows up?" Player personnel specialists can fool themselves into mediocrity. I wanted Willis to think about what could actually be done, given the player situation. I wanted to give him a sense of urgency. Would Derrick Coleman fit into the game plan for winning the championship? Maybe he could develop character and a work ethic, but it would be around the time that pigs learned to fly.

Answering the Question

I asked Willis what it would take to make the Nets a championship team. His bottom-line answer was money. That put the ball in my court. As president of the Nets and the person in charge of coming up with the money, I had to ask myself a different question: What's it gonna take to make our marketing department the best one of them all? That could bring in the money.

Before becoming president, I was the Nets' marketing consultant for two and a half years. In my second year as consultant, I asked Jim Leahy, vice president of ticket sales, this question: "What's it gonna take for the Nets to have the best ticket sales department in all of sports?"

"All the things we can't get," Leahy said.

"Let's make a list," I said.

We closed the door to his office and sat down, Leahy at his computer.

Leahy said that the first item on the list should be a better team.

"You can't have that," I said. "We work with the product we are given. The team has been awful in the past, and its near future looks awful. We market the team we're given. Now, under these circumstances, let's come up with a list of what it's gonna take to become the best ticket sales department in all of sports this year."

Here's what we came up with:

1. **More salespeople.** Northern New Jersey is a huge market. If you picked it up and dropped it into the state of Nebraska, it would be the eighth largest market in the country. It had 20,000 businesses we could count as targets. We determined that we should have one salesperson per 1,000 businesses. We had seven ticket salespeople, so we needed thirteen more. Leahy thought the owners would never approve that increase in overhead.

2. **A reasonable work environment.** Why did the Nets have only seven ticket salespeople? Because we had only seven work cubicles. The offices at that time were in the arena and there was no more available space. We would have to rent space outside the arena.

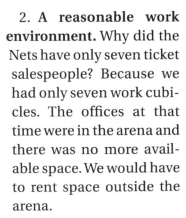

"The owners will never approve that," Leahy said.

"We're not passing judgment now on whether we can do it or not," I said. "We're just making a list of what it's going to take to have the best ticket sales department in all of sports. A reasonable work environment is one of those factors." He wrote it down on the list.

3. **Training, training, training, and when we were tired, more training.** We hired young people with little or no experience. And we hired cheap. Homeless people made more money. However, these kids wanted to "run away and join the circus" — get into pro sports — and we had the circus.

To be successful, we could not wait for these young salespeople to get better naturally. We had to accelerate their progress.

"I can get them started with a ticket sales boot camp," I told Leahy, "but the real burden falls on your shoulders. We need to train every day."

4. **More tools for the salespeople.** Most teams have their salespeople sell just season tickets. You know, buy a ticket to all the team's games or don't buy at all. That strategy might work for a team like the Chicago Bulls, which won six championships in eight years, but for most other teams it was self-defeating. "No problem," I told Leahy, "This one is the easiest thing on the list." We had already created some very popular ticket packages the year before. We would just create some more for specific corporate targets.

5. **Big-time database marketing.** We had started to collect names of people who we knew were interested in the Nets or the NBA. We needed to dramatically expand that

effort. It would take computers and a "Database King" — somebody who would stay up nights thinking of ways to expand the list.

That list doesn't seem too intimidating, does it? Not at all. Next, I asked Leahy to swap chairs with me. I started typing on his computer. We were going to prepare a case for the Supreme Court — not the nine Washington worthies in long robes, but the seven owners of the Nets. This document would be the key to becoming the number one ticket sales department.

We worked on the report for two days. It wasn't just typing; we needed to gather evidence. For instance, we knew the owners wouldn't agree to hire thirteen more salespeople and rent space for them without knowing the cost. We found space near the arena. We itemized the costs of salespeople, office, and phones. We projected sales. The whole report was only eight pages, but it answered every question, every objection that a naysayer could come up with. Then we rehearsed our oral presentation. We took this as seriously as if we were petitioning the real Supreme Court to save us from lethal injection.

Our plan was approved in two weeks. A year later, we had a ticket marketing machine. A year after that, we had the best ticket sales department in all of sports. In fact, it might have been the best ticket sales department that ever was and ever will be.

It all started with just one question: "What's it gonna take to become the best ticket marketing department in all of sports?" In the most hopeless situation you could find in sports — the New Jersey Nets — we had done it.

When You've Got Nothing

You know the one thing that most start-up companies don't have? Cash. When these start-ups think about advertising, they stop thinking about it a few seconds later. An advertising budget isn't something you think about as a start-up. Let's take this a step further. Suppose you're a start-up with little cash, and to make things worse it's a bad economy. Instead of heading for the hills, let's look at how this start-up from Austin, Texas, took steps forward.

The entrepreneur is a guy named Gary Keller, and he formed a real estate agency named Keller Williams Realty. They started in 1983 when mortgage rates were as high as 13 percent (ouch!).

Gary Keller asked his team the question: What's it gonna take to get people to visit our houses?

Money for advertising was, of course, not there for Keller Williams. No newspaper ads for them. No radio or TV. Instead of spending money that they didn't have, they made cheap yard signs. They blanketed the nearby expressway to promote open houses during the weekend. On Monday, the city workers came by and took down all the cheap signs, but the Keller Williams mission was accomplished. They had sold houses!

The "bandit" signs had worked. Back to making more hand-made signs. Four years later, Keller Williams was the number-one real estate agency in Austin, Texas.

Years later, Keller Williams offices were expanding all over the United States. To help increase their awareness in new territories Gary Keller asked his team: "What's it gonna take to make this company famous?"

They could have spent millions of dollars running quirky ads on the Super Bowl like Go Daddy. But Keller Williams built the business with no advertising. Instead of ads, he wrote three national bestsellers:

- *The Millionaire Real Estate Agent* (over 500,000 copies sold)

- *The Millionaire Real Estate Investor*

- *SHIFT: How Top Real Estate Agents Tackle Tough Times* (made the *New York Times, Wall Street Journal,* and *USA Today* bestseller lists)

These books have sold over one million copies! They are, of course, the perfect example of target marketing: they made Keller Williams famous to real estate agents across the country. When Keller Williams came recruiting, the company was as well known to real estate agents as the University of Texas, Southern Cal, Florida, or Notre Dame is to football prospects.

2008 and 2009 were the roughest years in the real estate industry in 70 years. Many Realtors were downsizing as fast as they could. In that time, Coldwell Banker had lost 12 percent of its agents; Century 21 had lost 21 percent; RE/MAX had lost 12.8 percent. Keller Williams had gained 8.3 percent!

Keller Williams is the third largest real estate company in the United States. By the time the ink dries on this book they could be number two; they're that close. And it all started with an outrageous idea of using cheap handmade signs instead of expensive advertising.

It's easy to ask the question, "What's it gonna take?" It's the answer that causes pain. I learned this as a consultant to troubled teams. If I asked business executives of pro sports teams, "What's it gonna take to be the best marketing department in the league this year?" I faced a lot of resistance. People would tell me in great detail why it wasn't possible. If I had debated them, I would have lost. They had hard evidence. After all, year after year they proved that what they were doing wasn't working and that there were plenty of valid reasons that it wasn't their fault.

When even the concept of asking "What's it gonna take?" makes executives get into a sumo's stance, I feel like sending them to Mexico. Why Mexico? Well, I understand they still allow lobotomies to be done. You know, drill a hole in the temple, stick in a screwdriver, stir it around, patch it up. But I'm a marketing guy, not a travel agent. I work with the product I'm given — and the people. Instead of sending them to Mexico, I get them to start making a list of what it's gonna take.

Two Small Favors

The whole purpose of this chapter is to get you to ask yourself just one question. You know the question. It depends, of course, on your situation. It could focus on your department:

What's it gonna take to be the best marketing department in our industry this year?

Or maybe it's about your company:

What's it gonna take to raise revenue in staggering amounts this year?

Here's the first favor I'll ask of you. Take the question that is most applicable to you and write it down on a 3 × 5 card. Or an envelope. Or a bar napkin. Any-thing you can put in your shirt pocket. Go ahead, write it down. I'll wait.

That's the first favor. The second favor's even easier. Whatever you wrote that question down on, put it in your shirt pocket. Go ahead, try it. Now, get used to that question in your shirt pocket. You need to have it there every day. You don't need to show it to anybody. This is just a little favor you are doing for me — our little secret.

Don't worry about answering that question right now. You'll come up with more and better answers as you read each chapter of this book. Believe me, the tough part isn't the answers. The tough part is asking yourself such a demanding question. Now that you've done that — and the question is tucked away safely in your shirt pocket — the rest is easy. Read on.

A SIMPLE TEST YOU CAN TAKE

There are only two questions to the simple test for this chapter. Don't blow it.

1. I wrote down the question "What's it gonna take to this year?" and placed it in my shirt pocket. (True/False)

2. We're already the best (department or company), so I don't need to write down that question and put it in my shirt pocket. (True/False)

Answers

1. I hope you did me that favor and circled True. If you didn't, you were probably intimidated by the question.

Or you just thought it was a silly exercise. Well, first of all, I didn't ask you if the question was reasonable. All I asked you was a favor — just write down the question and put it in your shirt pocket. You may consider the question unreasonable or impossible. For now, that's irrelevant. What's relevant is that you do me the favor.

If you are truly intimidated by the question, I'm willing to back off a little bit. Let me ask you the backup question:

What's it gonna take to _____ next year?

Notice how I'm giving you a little breathing room? It's not this year, it's next year. Now you've got some time.

So you still have time to ace this little test for chapter 2. Go ahead, write down the question. Place it in your shirt pocket. Mark your answer True.

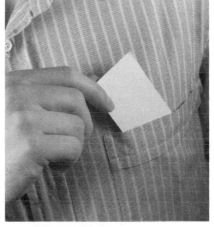

2. True. You don't have to write down the question and put it in your shirt pocket. All you have to do is think about the fact that some of your competitors may have written down the question, put it in their shirt pockets, and are now starting to think about how to steal some market share from you.

Can't happen? Heh, heh, heh. Remember when General Motors had 60 percent of the automobile market? Remember when IBM dominated the computer business? When Kodak had a 90 percent share in color film? When Xerox was becoming a generic name for copying? Nobody, but nobody, thought those companies would lose their dominance.

Now, after you've thought about this, read the second question again. See if you can come up with a different answer.

P.S. What's It Gonna Take to Have Outrageous Customer Service?

The Dayton Dragons, a Single-A minor-league baseball team, started its games in 2000. For the one hundred years before that, no team in the history of minor-league baseball had sold every ticket to every game during a season. That, of course, piqued my interest. What if we applied the same marketing principles that we did in the NBA to the Dayton Dragons? Why wouldn't we sell out?

We felt we could market our way to selling every seat to every game during the first season. Subsequent sellout seasons, however, required more. We needed a secret weapon. The secret weapon was outrageous customer service.

In planning before that first season, we asked ourselves one serious question: What's it gonna take to have the best customer service in all of sports? *Outrageous customer service!*

Marketing was going to deliver us sellouts in the first year; customer service was going to deliver us sellouts in the following years.

Keep in mind that the frontline troops in our customer service were mostly part-time employees like ushers and food service people. Some of the workers were retired. Many of these people had day jobs. They would work a full day someplace else, and then come to work for us. If they had a bad day at work, it would be easy for them to take out their frustration with our customers.

Here's some of the things we did:

1. **Your responsibility to buy dropped ice cream.** If any employee, whether an usher or the team president, saw a fan drop an ice cream (or soda or hot dog or beer), it was the employee's responsibility to offer to buy a replacement product right away. The usher or president would spend his or her own money and then be reimbursed at the end of the game. No receipts were necessary. That may sound too lenient, too open for scams, but if one employee was allegedly buying 200 replacement ice cream cones, we'd probably figure it out.

2. **No thick customer service manual.** Instead, we used a wall. That's right a wall. We tried to impress upon our part-time employees that they were empowered to do "whatever it takes to solve a fan's problem." That's right, whatever it takes. How in the world would we explain that in real terms? A thick manual might do it, but, alas, nobody would read it. Our fans could tell our part-time employees about great customer service. For instance, we got a letter from a lady who had brought her elderly mother to a game. After the game, they were slowly navigating their way out. One of the ushers asked if he could help. He helped guide them to their car a block away. That letter, blown up to poster size, went up on the wall in the employees' locker room. It joined six other letters, each one distinct in telling how an usher helped a fan. So, when we got a new employee, we said that it was his or her responsibility to do "whatever it takes to solve a fan's problem." For guidelines, "read the wall" and then take a quick True/False quiz. That was our customer service manual.

3. **Choice tickets for free, and you get paid.** There were times that our ushers just wanted to attend one of our games as a fan. We made that possible. We had eight season tickets that we dedicated to our part-time employees.

They'd sign up for the games they wanted to attend. So they wouldn't lose a payday, we also *paid them* the nights they went to the games as a fan. (There were a couple of rules here: the part-time employee just couldn't give the tickets away and not attend the game. These tickets were for the employees and their families and friends, so they should enjoy the game with them.)

4. **Free gifts.** During the season, we would give various gifts to our ticket package buyers. You know, bobbleheads or baseballs or hats. We made sure that our part-time employees also received those gifts.

There was a lot more that we did for our part-time employees that worked our games, but you get the idea.

The results?

Well, first of all, we had a bunch of part-time employees that were an absolute delight to be with.

And we received thousands of letters and e-mails from fans that were enthralled with our customer service. The unusual things our employees did. Some of those things actually made the wall.

And yes, we did sell out every ticket to every game in that first year. Then the sellout string continued year after year after year. Sometime in 2011, the Dayton Dragons will break the sellout string of 814 games by the Portland Trail Blazers (from 1977–1991).

Marketing gave us that first year of sellouts. Asking "What's it gonna take to have the best customer service in all of sports?" led us to all the following years of sellouts.

CHAPTER 3

Pushing the Outrageous Envelope

Picture this: You're presenting a serious marketing idea, and everyone in the audience falls down laughing. Rolling in the aisle.

That's the kind of idea I've always looked for. In fact, when I was president of the New Jersey Nets, we had a page in our company manual that said: If people fall down laughing when you present an idea, that idea has *a chance* of becoming a breakthrough idea. When an idea is so outrageous that it causes people to laugh at the idiocy of it, then it's time to push the outrageous envelope and see if that idea can be developed.

I pushed such an envelope when I met George Lois.

George Lois is a legendary ad guy in New York City who has written a bunch of books on advertising. One of my favorites is his book *What's the Big Idea?*

"What could you do to get people to talk about the Nets?" George asked me. "Do you know how hard it is to get people to talk about a company? Usually you have to do something awful — like poison somebody or crash an oil tanker. Boy, then they talk! But how can you get people to talk about you guys, to forget the team's sordid past, to think it might be fun to attend your games?"

"I don't know, George, we're working on it."

"Jockstraps," he said.

"What?" I said.

"Jockstraps."

George recommended that we hand out jockstraps to every man, woman, and child who came to our games. Every home game, all season long. You'd get a jockstrap every time you came through the turnstile. If you went to our full slate of forty-one home games, you'd have forty-one jockstraps.

Now that sounded really outrageous. Even for me.

I didn't laugh. I was stunned. And that was good. An idea that stuns you instead of making you laugh stands a good chance of being a breakthrough idea.

As George described the idea, I didn't have any trouble visualizing the results. People would be shocked. But some would think it was funny, maybe even cute. Especially the women; they would find a home for that free jockstrap — either with the man they had attended the game with or somebody at work.

("Here's your jock," says the woman, handing it to a male coworker.

"What?" he says, thinking, Did I leave that somewhere I shouldn't have?

"I got it at the Nets game," she says.)

After I recovered from the shock, I drove back to my office and shut my door. I thought about George's crazy idea. Then I posed the outrageous opportunity to a few staffers.

They laughed.

Ah-hah, we have a chance, I thought. A chance for a breakthrough idea.

I did some numbers on the cost. We had a great contact who could get things made in Taiwan, cheap. Every year he sold us 100,000 baseball caps at ninety cents each. A jock wouldn't cost that much, would it? I asked our contact for a quote on jocks.

"What size?" he asked.

"Large," I said, "All large." The packaging, of course, would say Extra Large.

The price came back: around $2 each, more than twice the cost of the cap.

"It's the packaging," our contact explained. "Hats don't need to be individually packaged. The jock costs about as much to package as to make. It's also more complicated."

We were expected to sell over 600,000 tickets that season. At $2 each, we'd be spending over $1 million for jocks. We didn't have that kind of money. If we had, we'd have spent it on another lousy player.

Normally, when you push the outrageous envelope and come to a speed bump, you pull back the envelope. Instead, I redirected the envelope.

I looked at our schedule. We had only seven home games in November. If we gave every man, woman, and child a jock for just the November home games, that would be only 100,000 straps — $200,000. We didn't have that much either, but it was more doable than the million dollars.

Even with the idea scaled back, we'd still get the outrageous lift. It would get people talking about the Nets, and we wouldn't even have to sink an oil tanker.

I talked to the staff again. Some were still appalled. That was a good sign. Others started to like the idea; that was also a good sign.

The next speed bump turned out to be our jockstrap supplier. "We'll need six months," he said.

"Six months? We get hats in three months!"

"Everybody in Taiwan makes hats. Just stitch in your logo. No problem. Jockstraps are far more complicated. Nobody makes jockstraps."

Six months to deliver jockstraps meant February or March instead of November. "How about doing it for the playoffs?" our contact asked. For most teams, that might have worked. But we were competing to be the worst team in the NBA, not a playoff team. So I pulled the outrageous envelope back and stuck it in a drawer.

Before the next season rolled around, I left the Nets, so the outrageous jockstrap idea stayed in the drawer. However, somewhere, sometime, you'll hear about a team that gives a jockstrap to every man, woman, and child who attends a game. It won't matter if that team isn't in your neck of the woods. You'll still want to go see it and get your free jock. Extra Large.

Getting Past Bland

I think we're all conditioned to think bland.

Bland is safe. Bland is politically correct. Bland is not getting laughed at.

Bland, however, is bad marketing.

Bland doesn't make the buyer think. Bland doesn't touch the emotions of buyers. Bland doesn't motivate the buyer to buy. But marketing bland is popular. Let me reiterate why bland is popular:

- Bland is safe.

- Bland is politically correct.

- Bland is not getting laughed at.

Marketing bland does work, however. It works when competing against other bland marketing. Then, whoever has the biggest pile of bland usually wins.

Marketing bland, however, doesn't work against Marketing Outrageously. In fact, against Marketing Outrageously, marketing bland isn't safe at all — it's dangerous to those who use it. Marketing Outrageously beats the hell out of marketing bland, time after time after time. We'll cover a lot of examples in this book.

What Do You Mean, Push?

Taking the step to marketing bland is easy; it's the way we've been trained to think. Marketing Outrageously is harder. We can be thankful for that. If it were easy, it would be much tougher to compete.

The first step to Marketing Outrageously, though, seems easy. You just shut yourself in your office. That's easy enough, right?

In the peace and privacy of your own office, look over your left shoulder. Then look over your right shoulder. Look for hidden cameras. When you're sure you're alone, take an outrageous marketing idea — like George Lois's idea about jockstraps — and write it down on a piece of paper. Put that piece of paper in an envelope. On the envelope, write a few words to identify the idea, like "free jockstraps." Place that outrageous envelope on your desk, right in front of you. Now push the outrageous envelope a few inches away from you — not too far.

Now: Did anyone chop off your hand when you touched the envelope?

Of course not. You're alone in your office. You're safe. Nobody there to yell, "Look at this stupid idea!" Now you can start to examine that outrageous idea, just as I did George's crazy jockstrap idea. In the safety of your office, you can imagine the boost your company will get from your outrageous idea. You can visualize the upside.

Now: Physically push the envelope a bit farther. Hear that? Amazing, isn't it? You can actually hear the negatives in your mind.

When I pushed the envelope on free jockstraps, I heard my first negative: "People will be offended."

I visualized my answer: "We offend people now. We offend everybody who comes to our games. Our players are awful. They don't try. They're always complaining. But this jockstrap thing could be fun. It could be more entertaining than our players. It could be outrageous."

Another negative popped up: "Our fans will throw the jockstraps on the floor."

"We give away basketballs, we give away caps, we give away gym bags. They don't throw those on the floor. Why would anybody throw a jock?"

Pushing a real envelope in the safety of your office is a terrific exercise to help you to examine an outrageous idea. Think of it as a dress rehearsal in which you play both parts — advocate and naysayer. As an advocate, you can think up good reasons to do it. As a naysayer, you may come across some legitimate objections. Answer the objections yourself. I did. I contacted our Taiwan supplier to find out how much those jockstraps would cost. In other words, I pushed the envelope a little further.

Start Testing the Idea

Once you've gone through that dress rehearsal, you might want to try the idea on some staff members. Not in a staff meeting or with your boss present — it's just too easy for everybody to think safe and bland and fill the air with reasons why not. It's better to approach a staff member casually, one on one, off the record.

And, at least initially, it's better to lay the blame on somebody else.

"Do you want to hear a crazy idea?" you could say to a staff member or friend in the industry. "This is really nuts. It came from George Lois. Crazy guy. Remember how we had been talking about how we could get people talking about us? A ten-game winning streak is, of course, out of the question. Well, George suggested that we hand out a jock to every man, woman, and child who attends our games. Would that get people talking?"

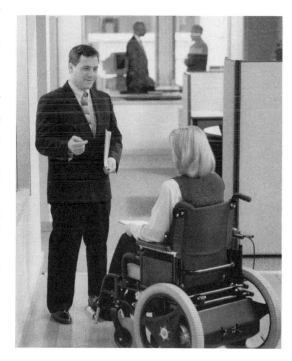

You may feel uncomfortable the first few times you try this. That's why you should blame somebody else. Relax. This wasn't your idea, it was crazy George's.

You may also find out that people won't know how to respond to you. They might not know whether you're serious about the idea or not. That's okay. Just go on to the next question:

"What do you think is the possible upside for this crazy idea of George's?"

The initial answer will probably be negative. That's okay, too. After all, we've been trained to think bland. It's not our nature to evaluate an outrageous idea.

When you get a negative reply, answer it this way: "I know about that problem, but I was just thinking about the possible upside. Forget about the negatives for a minute — what's the possible upside?"

Do It Again

You don't remember the first time you tried to walk. You fell on your face.

You probably don't remember the first time you tried to hit a baseball. You missed.

But you'll remember the first time you bring up an outrageous idea. It won't fly.

That's okay. Do the drill again.

Go to your office. Close the door. Check for hidden cameras. Pick out an envelope. Place it in front of you. Write

down a few words about an outrageous marketing idea like "free jockstraps." Now, push it away from you. As you think about it, inch it farther and farther away from you.

Try the idea out on some of your staff. The second or third or fourth time you do this, you will get better answers. When they think of the possible upside, they'll think less of the negatives and more of the positives. These outrageous ideas won't seem as — well — outrageous to them. They'll think more often that an outrageous idea is doable.

How to Be Known as Well as Kobe or Elvis

There are some people that are famous enough that they can go with just one name. For instance, even if you're not an NBA fan, you would know who LeBron is. Or Kobe. Think back: know who Elvis was? Go back even further, how about Liberace? Even with his off-course troubles, folks don't have trouble identifying who Tiger is.

Now let's look at the most unlikely company to leapfrog into one-name heaven, and how an outrageous marketing idea catapulted them to that position.

The company: American Family Life Assurance Company. Up until ten years ago, they were a sleepy insurance company from Columbus, Georgia, that was comfortably profitable. They had name recognition of 10 percent. Besides a name recognition problem, they had a problem with people recognizing what business they were in.

Dan Amos, the CEO, had the epiphany that they just had to get better name recognition, and then go from there.

He solicited recommendations from several ad agencies. One wanted to use Ray Romano as the spokesperson. Not bad. Another ad agency gathered its creative folks and sat by the lake in New York's Central Park, waiting for inspiration. They heard the ducks quacking. The quacking eerily sounded like Aflac's name. Voilà!

So, here's how this conservative Southern insurance company that nobody heard of — and if they had heard of them, they didn't remember the name — came face to face with a duck.

It took guts to use the duck as your "spokesperson." Lots of guts. Think of how the board of directors reacted to the idea!

If naysayers ever wanted to stand in line to kill an idea, this was it.

"We're a *serious* company," one naysayer surely said.

"A duck makes us a joke," another naysayer, agreeing with the first, would have said.

"My God, what will Wall Street think?" a third naysayer might have said.

Was the duck an outrageous idea? You better believe it. It would have been far easier to just laugh it off, chuckling about these silly advertising folks.

Dan Amos, the CEO, persevered, however.

In the first three years, with the duck leading the way, Aflac's sales *doubled.* Now it has annual increases of 12 to 15 percent of new sales. In ten years, the company's name recognition catapulted to 94 percent, on par with Nike and McDonald's.

Do You Have the Guts?

I was reluctant to use Aflac as an example because it was a national ad campaign that catapulted Aflac's name recognition.

A naysayer could easily say, "Just throw millions of dollars into a national ad campaign and it will work." While I think the naysayer would be wrong on that, and I could easily beat that naysayer in a debate, I'm not going to debate it here. The whole point of what I've written is the thought process that Aflac went through and then the guts it took to breathe life into it. That's what's important: *the thought process and the guts!*

WITNESS PROTECTION PROGRAM

Here's another example, and it did not include any advertising dollars to make it work.

I used this approach in creating some outrageous marketing to help a sleepy, Triple-A, minor-league baseball team in the glitz and entertainment capital of the world — Las Vegas. The Las Vegas Stars competed against all this glitz with — nothing. If you made a list of the five most boring things to do in this world, you'd put going to a Stars game somewhere on that list. The Stars did nothing to entertain the fans except play baseball. No music, no mascots, no promotions. That would be okay if there were a horde of hardcore baseball fans in Las Vegas, but there wasn't.

Mandalay Sports Entertainment purchased the team, then hired me as a consultant to ramp up revenues in staggering amounts. To do that, we would have to at least be *entertaining*. After all, why would people come out and spend money just to be bored? They could stay home and be bored for free.

It's pretty easy to be entertaining at a minor-league baseball game. However, for eighteen years the Stars had managed to be boring. How in the world could we convince the residents of Las Vegas that seeing this Triple-A baseball team could be fun? One way would be to send the team into a sports version of the witness protection program — change the name. With a new name — perhaps even an outrageous one — we might also change their boring identity.

I didn't just blurt this witness protection idea out to Mandalay. First, I asked various employees what they thought of the "Stars" name.

"I've always hated it," one employee of sixteen years said. "But that was the name of the team when I joined up."

"We're not really the stars," another employee said. "The stars of Las Vegas are the entertainment headliners at the casinos. We're a Triple-A baseball team. Very few of our players will even make it to the bigs."

After work, I went back to the privacy of my hotel room, where I pushed the outrageous envelope. I didn't have a specific name I was interested in; I pushed the envelope just on the concept of changing the name.

I pushed the envelope a little further. In that push, I realized that what was needed was a dramatic — even *controversial* — name. It had to get people talking. I pushed the envelope again.

A few weeks later, I gathered a few employees for a spontaneous meeting.

I said, "Suppose, just suppose, we *had* to change the name of the team. What would we call it?" I stood by the blackboard, ready to write down names — and was surprised by a flurry of ideas tossed at me faster than I could write. A lot of the names featured some facet of gambling — you know, One-Eyed Jacks, Whales (big bettors), Players, Sharks (as in card sharks). We got bogged down in these, so I suggested we steer away from gambling. After a few moments of silence, we picked up steam again.

One name seemed to jump out at us: the "51s" — as in Area 51, the supersecret air force base about 100 miles north of Las Vegas, the very existence of which the government denies. Area 51 is where the air force developed its stealth bomber and where — rumor has it — the United States is trying to reverse engineer a captured alien spaceship.

"Aliens and spaceships," one of the employees said. "It seems every third movie that's made has aliens and spaceships. Kids love that stuff; families love that stuff."

"It's *Star Wars.* It's *E.T.*"

"We could cut crop circles in the outfield," another said.

"Let's see what this would look like," I said, wanting us to push the outrageous envelope together. I suggested we hire a graphic artist to do a rendering. The artist, a whacko guy named John Masse, hit it the first time.

Our little ad hoc group met again. It seemed that everybody loved it. Except for one. "I hate it," this person said. "I like the idea of aliens and spaceships, but I hate the name 51s."

I thought that was a good sign. To get a breakthrough idea, there have to be some people who really hate it. If everybody loved it, I might have lost my enthusiasm.

We pushed the envelope a little further. The media got wind of it. Predictably, they hated it. Now I was sure we were on the right track.

Within two months, we officially made the name change. At that time of the year, December, the team had never before been mentioned in the media. The 51s, however, were featured in *Sports Illustrated, Time, USA Today,* the *New York Times,* and over 100 other newspapers in the United States. The 51s were even featured in the *Yomiuri Daily* in Tokyo.

The local newspaper, the *Las Vegas Review-Journal,* invited its readers to vote on its website whether they liked the name or not. The biggest response they had ever received before was 12,000 votes on the Binion murder trial, which, at that time, was as big in Las Vegas as O. J. was in the nation at large. The 51s received over 15,000 votes — and to our surprise, over 77 percent liked the name!

People were starting to think that maybe this Triple-A baseball team wouldn't be boring. Folks from around the country thought it was pretty good. The Las Vegas 51s went from 89th in licensed product sales in Minor League Baseball to number two!

The following year attendance zoomed upwards; sponsorship revenue doubled.

A couple of years later we sold the team. The new ownership didn't push the craziness of the name; in fact, I occasionally hear stories that they might change the name. Want to make any side bets that the new name won't be nearly as much fun? Or sell nearly as many caps?

PUTTING THE OUTRAGEOUS ENVELOPE IN THE VAULT

There are times when the outrageous idea never leaves my office. I push the outrageous envelope, and it looks like it has

potential. I push it further, and it looks even better. I push it one last time, and I spot some serious flaws. When the flaws are too serious, I just put the outrageous idea in the vault. All this can happen before I even discuss the idea with staffers.

There are also times I've discussed an outrageous idea with staffers, and we have examined the upside, measured the risks, decided it's a go situation, but at the last minute, just before breathing life into it, pulled the envelope back. That's what we did with George Lois's jockstrap idea.

When we pull the envelope back, I don't feel remorseful at all. I feel good, because in pushing it as far as we can, we not only uncover a lot of potential problems but we discover even more potential benefits. And there are times when it would be wrong to give the envelope that one last nudge into reality. However, when you push the outrageous envelope and at least demonstrate that you're serious about it, the staff learns how to think outrageously, how to bring outrageous ideas to the brink.

Occasionally we pushed an idea past the brink and enjoyed uncommon success with it. Other times, the outrageous idea went into the vault — a file cabinet, a CD, or the trash can. Many outrageous ideas have real merit but need better timing. These may eventually come back out of the vault and produce monster results.

The fun is in pushing the outrageous envelope. Many executives miss this kind of fun, and the outrageous success it can bring, because they don't even try. After all, it's too outrageous.

A SIMPLE TEST YOU CAN TAKE

1. Which would you rather do?
   a. Breathe life into outrageous marketing ideas that can give your company an increase of revenue in staggering amounts.
   b. Use a bland marketing program that works only if your competitor markets bland.
   c. Never have anybody fall down laughing at one of your marketing ideas.

2. Marketing Outrageously may work in the sports world, but it doesn't work in my industry, a very conservative industry. (True/False)

3. I'll try the "pushing the outrageous envelope" drill at least five times to see what happens. (True/False)

Answers

1. a. I hope you answered "a." Believe me, it's much more fun to market outrageously than to market bland — and far more rewarding for your company and for you. It's not as difficult to get into as you might think. Once you decide to try it out, your antennae will soon pick up your first outrageous idea. Do the drill: "push the outrageous envelope" in the privacy of your office. When you've pushed the envelope long enough to feel safe with it, push it outside your office with some staffers. Push gently. Then try it again. After a few pushes, you'll see that outrageous ideas are coming to you more naturally. You're on the brink now of a true breakthrough idea.

2. False. Marketing Outrageously works in any industry. In fact, the more conservative the industry, the bigger upside Marketing Outrageously will have. Go ahead, try it — "push the envelope" in the safety of your own office.

3. True! What have you got to lose? Go in your office. Close the door. Do the drill at least five times. Go ahead, really push it. I guarantee that you will come up with at least one outrageous idea that will make it out your door to staffers who will breathe life into it. It will bring you and your company great benefits. Caution: Trying the drill just once won't work. There's a learning curve. But if you try it five times, at least one run-through will pay off — big.

CHAPTER 4

Who Are You, Anyway?

It started with a cup of coffee I was having with Norm Sonju, president and general manager of the Buffalo Braves. I was the Braves' new vice president in charge of marketing. It was an awesomely bad team. The media were beating us up pretty good (we were on our way to winning just twenty-seven games out of eighty-two). There was daily speculation as to which city we were going to move to.

A little background: Two years before I joined up, the Braves had been a good team, exciting to watch. They had the league's top scorer, Bob McAdoo. Attendance lagged, however, and the owner threatened to move the team to Florida unless the business community supported them. The threat worked. Businesses bought a record number of season tickets. Whereupon the owner cashed the checks and, two days before the season opener, traded off McAdoo and other top starters for cash and sold the corpse of the organization to a new owner, KFC magnate

John Y. Brown. Season ticket holders were less than pleased. Speculation was not on whether, but when and where, the team would be moved. One newspaper columnist even wrote that we were a disgrace and an embarrassment to Buffalo and that we should move even before the season ended. You could practically smell the tar heating up and see the fans collecting feathers. This wasn't what you would consider a "Save the Braves for Buffalo" campaign.

I said to Norm, "I've been thrown out of better places than Buffalo. I want to sell out the last game."

Norm looked at me incredulously and said, "How are you going to do that?" He could practically hear the gears moving in my head. Then he said, "Don't tell me. Don't tell me a thing. Just do it." I guess that's like the president of the United States disavowing anything the CIA does.

I decided to bring Elvis Presley back to life. Elvis had died the year before, and now a lot of imitators were popping up. A friend of mine, Joe Weidensall, told me about one of the better ones, a guy named Eddie Brandon from Oklahoma. Joe had just finished producing a syndicated forty-hour radio special on Elvis for Westwood One and had seen Eddie perform. "Eerie, man," Joe told me. "Really eerie."

I cut a deal with Eddie. Then I set up a title sponsorship deal with the local Budweiser distributor for a special event: "Budweiser Presents a Tribute to the King of Rock and Roll, and the Buffalo Braves versus the New York Knicks." That's right, Elvis got lead billing. The sponsorship included a lot of newspaper ads and radio commercials to promote the event.

We brought Eddie in three days before the event. I didn't let him leave his hotel room, but we did extensive phone interviews on country-and-western radio stations. Eddie's impersonation wasn't just on stage; he was Elvis all the time. He not only sounded like Elvis, I believe he thought of himself as Elvis's reincarnation. When you had a cup of coffee with Eddie, it was like having a cup of coffee with Elvis.

Elvis Sighted in Buffalo!

The night before the performance, Eddie said he was getting cabin fever and needed to get out of his room. I didn't want to spoil the illusion and have people see him before the event, so I took him to a small piano bar in the suburbs. It was so dark in there you wouldn't recognize former president Richard Nixon if he was sitting next to you.

This was the type of piano bar that was a precursor to karaoke. At the back of the club was a microphone where, if you chose, you could sing the words to the song being played on the piano. Because it was so dark, I didn't see Eddie get up and walk to the microphone — I just heard Elvis singing in the dark.

But I could see the piano player's face lit by a lamp over the sheet music. He was stunned.

After the song, I heard Elvis/Eddie ask, out of the darkness, "Sir, do you know the 'American Trilogy'?" The piano player nodded and started to play. Elvis would have been proud.

When Eddie had finished, he got a standing ovation. I was standing and jumping and hollering with the rest of the people. "More! More!"

The next night, we sold out the arena. They were mostly Elvis fans. How do I know? Because Eddie's show began after the game ended. The game started with 8,000 fans in the arena. At halftime there were 12,000. When Eddie went on, we had over 19,000 seats filled.

That last night was a lot of fun. We lost the game, but we had sold every seat in the house. It was then that I started to think that pro sports teams had wrongly positioned themselves. For instance, we had thought we were in the basketball team business, but we were really in the entertainment business. Our entertainment happened to be pro basketball games.

This probably doesn't sound like much of a jump now, but it was a big leap at the time. Teams felt they had two responsibilities: play the games, and sell tickets to fans who clearly wanted to come to the games. Everything else was either irrelevant or a bother. Games on local radio or TV? That was considered nice public relations, as long as it didn't cost anything.

The next season, when I moved to Portland and became vice president of marketing with the Trail Blazers, I took the new positioning philosophy with me. The idea was not simply to bring in an Elvis impersonator or some halftime vaudeville or music act. These were only a small part of the picture. The important thing was our goal: to provide entertainment. This could include developing our own lucrative radio and television shows and magazines.

The Portland Trail Blazers were the first pro sports team to make this paradigm shift. Most other pro teams followed suit eventually, but you could say it all started with Elvis in Buffalo, New York.

Fly the Wabash Cannonball

Have you ever heard of the Erie Lackawanna Airline?

How about the Baltimore & Ohio Airline?

Denver & Rio Grande Western Airline?

Pennsylvania Airline? Wabash Airline? Santa Fe Airline?

Those were all railroad companies that positioned themselves in the railroad business. What if they had thought they were in the business of transporting people and goods? When air travel started to emerge as a reasonable alternative to trains for both people and shipping, the railroads had everything necessary to dominate that new industry. They had the financial clout, they had the credibility, they knew about schedules and timetables, about transporting people, about shipping. They were lacking in just two things: they didn't know how to fly planes, and they didn't have the vision about who they were. The flying could, of course, have easily been learned. But the railroads stayed locked in the belief that they were in the railroad business. This is the gist of Theodore Levitt's argument in his famous 1960 *Harvard Business Review* article, "Marketing Myopia."

What if the railroads had pushed the outrageous envelope? They might have positioned themselves in the transportation business. If they had, perhaps United and American would today be having to compete with the ATS Airline, otherwise known as the Atchison, Topeka, and Santa Fe. Maybe you'd be accumulating frequent flier miles on the Erie Lackawanna.

It's not just railroads, of course. You can look back and see where a lot of companies didn't know what business they were in. Smith-Corona was a major manufacturer of typewriters. Smith-Corona thought it was in the typewriter business. You can still buy typewriters, I think, but what if Smith-Corona had seen itself not in typewriters but in the word reproduction business? When computers came along, would Smith-Corona have followed its customers as they made the transition to personal computers? I think so.

Smith-Corona already had a retail network of stores that sold its typewriters. It had a sales staff. It had marketing people. Manufacturing typewriters is probably more com-

plex than assembling computers. If nothing else, Smith-Corona could have taken its brand name and developed a word processing software. After all, Microsoft Word and WordPerfect were created from scratch. But Smith-Corona didn't know what business it was in.

The Widest River

In 1995, a guy named his fledgling dot.com business after the world's widest river. The Amazon. This guy, Jeff Bezos, sold books on the Internet. How crazy was that? Just think of his competition. Besides the burgeoning Barnes & Noble and the aggressive Borders Books, you could get books anyplace. You could get books at the supermarket. At Walmart. At airports. And you could get books for free at libraries.

The results have been, of course, spectacular. In 2009, Amazon did almost $6 billion in book sales in the U.S. Barnes & Noble did $4.3 billion; Borders did $2.6 billion.

Amazon did this with no stores. All of their sales were over the Internet.

So, we can safely say that Amazon.com is in the book-selling business. Right? Ah, not so fast.

Amazon *utilized* books to build its base, but along the way they became America's *largest online retailer.* Their product lines now include: music CDs, videotapes and DVDs, tools, lawn and garden items, software, consumer electronics, toys and games, beauty products, clothing, groceries, and more.

Have they forsaken what got them there — books?

Of course not. In November 2007, Amazon rolled out its e-reader, Kindle. Just three years later, they sold 50 percent more digital books than hardcover books. It's been estimated that they sell 80 percent of the digital books bought.

So, did Jeff Bezos start out wanting to be the largest online retailer? I don't think so. He wanted to sell books. But as his Amazon.com attracted more and more customers, it was only natural to offer them other products.

Here's where he stole a page from eBay. eBay doesn't warehouse its products. eBay is a middleman. Basically, it's the same thing with Amazon.com. Most of its additional products are not bought by Amazon and then warehoused. Amazon just acts as a sales agent with no financial commitment to the supplier. It doesn't have the expense of inventory or warehousing for these products. Amazon provides *customers* — nowadays it gets 65 million customers to its U.S. website every month — and it takes a percentage of each of these sales.

Books are still the backbone of Amazon.com. It is aggressively building on that in its leadership efforts with digital books. But Amazon was opportunistic to extend its product line at very little additional cost. It's almost like walking down the street and just finding incremental sales laying there, waiting to be picked up.

The Acid Test

I arrived in Portland with the fresh understanding that the Trail Blazers were an entertainment company, and proceeded to run it that way. It worked to perfection. So what, said the naysayers; anything would work in Portland. After all, two years earlier, they had won an NBA title. Besides, they were the only pro team in town. I don't even debate those points. The real acid test for me wasn't Portland. Sure, we had done a lot of innovative sports marketing there, but the true test lay ahead of me.

I left the Blazers in 1989 when the owner, Larry Weinberg, sold the team to Microsoft cofounder Paul Allen. After the sale, I saw that things were going to change — for the better or for the worse — and since I had been a major architect in building our corporate culture of innovation, I didn't want to live with the new changes. It was time for me to ride on. After teaching college for a year at the University of Portland, I found myself consulting for the hapless, hopeless New Jersey Nets.

The Nets had been the worst team in the NBA for five straight years. They had the worst attendance in the NBA for those five years. They had a dismal past in the NBA and a scary future. So, armed with the concept that worked so well in Portland — that teams were in the entertainment business — I faced the challenge of finding something entertaining about the Nets.

Market Like Crazy

Somewhere along the line, a premise arose that if you had a great pro sports team you didn't have to market. The same premise is common in business — you know, build a better mouse-trap and they'll beat a path to your door. Well, that premise is false. I do admit, however, that if you have a lousy team, or a lousy product, you do have to work harder. With the Nets, we had to market like crazy.

Before we could think about entertaining all the fans we were going to attract, we had to figure out a way to get them to the arena. The best way, of course, would be to win games. Unfortunately, with the Nets, that wasn't a realistic option. So we targeted two marketing factors we thought might work in our favor:

1. **The NBA's megastars.** In the early 1990s, three of the NBA's all-time greats were playing — Larry Bird, Magic Johnson, and Michael Jordan. Everybody likes to see star performers at work, so we created seven-game ticket packages that let you do just that, about one game a month. We hoped this would at least give fans a chance to identify with our cast of characters.

2. **Families.** We felt we could attract families if the price were right. We sold a sponsorship to White Castle hamburger restaurants for a family ticket package — four tickets, four meals at White Castle, a Nets cap, and a Nets basketball for just $39.95. There was just one White Castle game per month, usually a weekend game against an opponent nobody wanted to see. But it was an offer families couldn't refuse. Every time we ran a White Castle family night, we sold out the arena.

By marketing like crazy, we brought the Nets up from last in attendance to twelfth in the league — from no sellouts to twenty-seven. Now we had to think about entertaining all these potentially loyal fans well enough to keep them coming back. How would we do that? We decided to work on the overall fan experience.

When fans came to the games, they would encounter two things they hadn't experienced before: a full house, and entertainment. The entertainment wasn't always our team, to be sure; it was the experience of attending a game in a sold-out arena and watching the superstars on the other teams do their magic.

To improve the ambiance of our games and make the events more inviting, we enhanced fans' experiences in several areas:

- **The excitement of arrival.** We rented huge search-lights, the kind you see at movie premieres, and turned them on full blast. If you were driving down the New Jersey Turnpike approaching the game, you'd see them miles away. You couldn't help feeling you were coming to a really big event.

- **Fancy tickets.** We changed our tickets to a large, Super Bowl–style format, with a full-color action picture on the front — not always our own players. The ticket made a neat souvenir.

- **Special effects.** During the national anthem, we turned down the lights, and when the singer sang, ". . . and the rockets' red glare, the bombs bursting in air," we set off fireworks.

- **The amazing visible announcer.** Instead of a disembodied voice, our announcer, Tim McLoone, was a presence on court, introducing players, directing promotions during timeouts, at other times appearing in the spotlight high in the stands.

- **Culture warp.** In the second half of the game, during a timeout, we sent two guys dressed up in huge sumo wrestler costumes racing from one end of the court to the other. Maybe this sounds silly — and it certainly was — but our Sumo Racers were often more popular than our players.

The ambiance we created didn't, by itself, draw people to the games. Good marketing did that. But once they had bought a ticket, we wanted fans to remember the experience fondly.

A couple of years after I left the Nets, the team hired a new head coach: John Calipari, from the University of Massachusetts. Then they paid a fortune for new players. The team started to play pretty well. They made the playoffs and faced Michael Jordan and the Chicago Bulls in the first round.

As they improved on the court, management began to phase out the extracurricular entertainment we had created. No more searchlights outside the arena. No more indoor fireworks. Alas, no more Sumo Racers. Now the Nets were reverting to being a basketball team, dependent on winning lots of games, at the mercy of losses and injuries. The new

premise was the old false premise: If you have a great team, you don't have to market.

Think about that. As a marketer, would you want your job to hang on the bounce of a ball?

Potential Magic

There are mystical, magical opportunities out there for companies that push the outrageous envelope and recognize who they are and what business they are in. When you know what business you're in, those opportunities just naturally surface. If Smith-Corona had felt it was in the word processing business, would it have been that big a leap for them to get into computers? Of course not. It would have been a natural evolution of their typewriter business.

Look at history. Look at the railroads. Look at Smith-Corona. Look at Amazon.com. Look at your own company. What business are you really in?

A SIMPLE TEST YOU CAN TAKE

1. (Fill in the two empty lines.)

	Railroads	Smith-Corona	Your company
Business they thought they were in	Railroading	Typewriters	_____
Perspective they should have had	Transporting people and goods	Word processing	_____

2. It's easy to change a company's perspective of what business it is in. (True/False)

3. It's not a marketing function to change the company's perspective. (True/False)

Answers

1. Don't think that this question is a waste of time. Let me explain.

I'm not a big fan of mission statements for companies. Often these are ponderously written and then never read again by anybody. However, I'm a great believer in knowing what business you're really in. When you truly know that, it pervades everything you do.

A friend of mine owned a business magazine that had been in publication for over 100 years. I asked him what business he thought he was in. "The magazine business," he replied.

"Wrong," I said. "You are in the branded information business."

He asked me to explain.

"When you're in the magazine business," I said, "you sell subscriptions, you sell advertising, and you print a magazine every week or every month. When you're in the branded information business you're in the highly lucrative seminar business, you're in the Internet, you're into cable shows about business. You can provide information under your 'brand name,' whatever the medium — not just with ink and paper.

"Any of those activities could bring you more profit than just publishing a magazine every week or every month. You could look at the magazine as a promotional tool that by itself makes a profit and that drives business to the other opportunities. Opportunities in these other fields will naturally come because you publish a magazine. You're in the branded information business."

When you identify which business you're really in, your marketing is much sharper and more effective, and you open yourself up to opportunities you would never have recognized before.

2. False. If it were easy to change your perspective on what business you're truly in, you can be sure at least one railroad would have taken the plunge and become an airline. The resistance must have been tremendous. When I went to the Portland Trail Blazers, I sure didn't find it easy to change the perspective. It took years.

3. False. The easy answer might be that "it's not my job, man." Yep, it's the CEO's, not the marketing person's. However, who is going to be most affected if the company doesn't recognize what business it's really in? These days, it's usually not the CEO. If everything goes to hell in a handbasket, the CEO usually has a golden parachute. You're the marketing person? Hey, our sales went down under your watch. See ya!

My feeling is that you, as the marketing person, have to figure it out on behalf of the company. Sure, you might find resistance at the top to embracing your new perspective, but you can work it from the inside. What if the marketing manager at Smith-Corona had understood that S-C was really in the word processing business? That marketing manager

could have researched the computer business in its infancy and, over time, built a logical case for making the transition to personal computers. If that case were rejected, then the marketing person would know it was time to ride on before the posse came into town. When a company fails to understand its business, the posse always rides in with guns a-blazing.

CHAPTER 5

Get Caught Up in Revenue

I was walking along the beach in Maui, trying to relax and not succeeding. A stress knot that felt as big as a golf ball had cramped my back. Here I was in Paradise, getting away from a grueling season with the Trail Blazers, getting recharged to go back to Portland for the next season, and I couldn't even enjoy myself.

I needed to relax. We were going to introduce some new concepts in Portland. These ideas weren't new just to Portland, but to the entire sports industry. Big energy was going to be needed.

Then I saw a sign: Lomi-Lomi Hawaiian Massage. Just what I needed. Therapy from a beautiful Hawaiian girl.

I walked into the beach-front building. I looked around. It was a beauty shop. There was a woman. "Massage? Around there," she said, pointing at a room divider.

Behind the divider sat a Hawaiian guy reading a newspaper. He looked up and smiled. "Lie down here," he said. "On your stomach."

"I have a stress knot in my back," I said. "Can you work it out?"

"Sure, sure," he said. He began massaging my feet. Then he started to press hard on different spots on the soles of my feet. Really hard and really painful.

"No, no, no," I said. "Not my feet — my back, my back."

"Right," he said. "That's what I'm doing. You'll see."

How stupid was I? Instead of strolling along on a postcard-perfect Maui beach, I was letting this Hawaiian guy torture my feet. His name was Gene Clark, and his specialty was using lomi-lomi, reflexology, Swedish massage, and anything else he could think of to cause me pain.

Amazingly, though, as I lay there wincing while he kneaded the soles of my feet, I felt my back loosen up. The knot gradually dissolved. I began to relax.

"You have sinus problems, don't you?" Gene said.

"No, I don't have any sinus problems," I said. Sure, I got headaches, but that was just stress. Sinus problems meant runny nose, and I didn't have a runny nose.

"Oh, yeah," Gene said. He pressed a new spot on my foot, then another. Suddenly I felt as though someone had turned a valve in my nose. My sinuses began draining like a fire hose.

Gene handed me a tissue. "Feel more clear-headed?" Gene asked, smiling.

"Wow," I said, "I sure do."

I was amazed. I could touch the soles of my feet and just feel — well — feet. Gene could do it and diagnose a problem I didn't know I had.

I saw my feet as two things that would get me from Point A to Point B. Gene saw them as signs of my health. Apparently he could read these signs better than the doctor who gave me my annual physical. Nobody had ever before told me I had a sinus problem.

Business can be like that. Everything seems to be going smoothly, but suddenly, out of nowhere, disaster strikes. Most likely, the disaster has been building for a long time, but nobody at the company read the signs. Sure, I get headaches, but I don't have a sinus problem.

In almost any situation, if you read the warning signs early, you can devise a remedy that not only heads off disaster but jump-starts your company. You can find a lemon and turn it into lemonade — if you read the signs.

So lie on your stomach, imagine you're gazing at the beautiful Pacific Ocean, and let me press your feet.

EMERGENCY IN EDMONTON

The voice on the phone sure didn't sound like it came from the most hated man in the history of Canada. It was friendly, and even sort of cultured.

I hadn't been expecting his call. In fact, I hadn't been expecting any calls. Just the day before, I had resigned as president of the New Jersey Nets. It was early September 1995, and I was in my rented New Jersey home packing. My wife and I were returning to our real home in Portland, Oregon.

"Jon, this is Peter Pocklington of the Edmonton Oilers."

I knew the name, I had heard of the reputation. Peter was the man who, in 1988, had traded the greatest hockey player in the history of the world, Wayne Gretzky, to the Los Angeles Kings for $17 million cash and some players. He used part of the cash to build a twenty-foot-tall statue of Gretzky outside the arena. That was a nice tribute to Gretzky, but it also served as a reminder to fans that their idol had been sold for pieces of silver. Seventeen million pieces of silver.

Let's put that transaction into perspective. The only trade in the NBA that could equal it would involve Michael Jordan, the greatest basketball player ever. Think of the reaction if Chicago Bulls owner Jerry Reinsdorf had sold Michael Jordan to another team for cash. Reinsdorf would have easily been more notorious than mobster Al Capone. At least Scarface Al provided free food for the poor people.

That type of infamy didn't happen when Gretzky was traded. When Gretzky was becoming the greatest hockey player in the history of the National Hockey League, he was doing it without the massive media attention that had routinely focused on Jordan. The NHL in the 1980s had no national television deal in the United States. So Gretzky dominated the NHL in relative obscurity in the U.S. And did he dominate! He certainly dominated the NHL as much as Jordan dominated the NBA. Jordan won six championships in eight years; Gretzky won four championships in five years.

"I hear you're heading back to Portland, Oregon," Peter said.

News travels fast.

"On your way back to Portland, could you stop off at Edmonton?" Peter asked.

I laughed. "Peter, you don't just 'stop off' at Edmonton. That's like stopping off at Albuquerque."

This time Peter laughed. He might be hated, but he did have a sense of humor.

"I'm in trouble, Jon," Peter said, lowering his voice. "I don't want to move the Oilers, but I'm not sure we can survive in Edmonton. I need you to come to Edmonton to see if we have a chance."

I told Peter that I couldn't come to Edmonton. I was worn down after four and a half years taking the hapless, hopeless New Jersey Nets into profitability. After resigning from the Nets, the first and only thing on my agenda was to chill out. I begged off and went to Ireland with a good friend, Darrell Rutter.

In the mornings, I played golf; afternoons, wrote *Ice to the Eskimos;* evenings, had a few Guinnesses. When I got back to Portland, Peter called again. I told him I was still on vacation. This time I flew to Hawaii, played more golf, wrote some more, enjoyed sunset dinners with my wife. I was becoming an expert at chilling out.

The day after I got back from Hawaii, Peter called again. This time I agreed to go up to Edmonton.

The team was in awful financial shape. Since Gretzky had left, seven years before, the organization had fallen off a cliff. Season ticket sales were down to 5,500 from their peak of 14,000. There was red ink all over the place. All that wouldn't surprise you or me. After all, Peter had sold a legend for a lot of pieces of silver. Good things don't happen when you do that.

What did surprise me, however, was that there were signs of deterioration the summer after they won their first Stanley Cup. Now, remember, the Oilers won five Stanley Cups in seven years. That's an incredible record. But as soon as they had won the first one, they began to sell fewer season tickets.

This was a warning sign — and a sign of real opportunity — but nobody saw it. The opportunity was lost; disaster was inevitable.

I asked Peter why the number of season tickets declined after they won their first Stanley Cup. "Been there, done that," Peter said. "I think the fans felt the first Stanley Cup was enough."

The man who had put the dynasty together, Glen Sather, said the same thing. So did the marketing people.

In fact, after each year the Oilers won another Stanley Cup, the number of season tickets sold went down!

Been there, done that? Hogwash!

Back-to-back championships are tough to win. It's hard for teams to keep their focus. Players are not as hungry for the second title; they don't work as hard; key players become juicy prizes for other teams. Fans, however, are different. Once a team wins a championship, a bandwagon rolls along drawing in every man, woman, and child within reasonable driving distance. There's not a lot of this "been there, done that" crap with the fans. They just want more.

Winning the title actually obscured the fissures in the Oilers organization. There were clear signs that the Oilers were going to take a big tumble, but these signs were ignored. That first Stanley Cup was a powerful narcotic.

Footwork

I spent just an hour talking to Peter. When I consult with a team or a company, there are two areas I don't spend much time with in the beginning:

1. the brains (owners or top managers) or

2. the product.

It's not that the leaders or the product aren't important. Obviously they are. But I'm from the school that you market what you are given. If the brains aren't quite of the Einstein caliber, or if the product is mediocre or worse, you still have to market what you're given. So, like my Maui reflexologist friend Gene Clark, I start pushing pressure points on the feet — the sales staff.

When a company is struggling, you'll generally find certain things true of the sales staff:

• **Low morale.** This is usually because "we need a better product to sell." Salespeople would much prefer to sell the best product in the field. But how many of us really get to do that? It's up to the marketing people to position the less-than-best product correctly. After all, somewhere inside that ugly product is an absolute gem of a feature.

When salespeople sing the better-product lament, I usually suspect that the next two factors are stronger than they should be.

- **Inadequate training.** There's an easy way to find out how well a sales staff is trained. Pretend to be a prospect. Have each salesperson make a presentation to you. If you have a cruel streak, videotape each presentation. This slops on the pressure, but it provides vivid proof of how well the sales staff have been trained. (Bigger companies usually do a pretty good job of training. It's those with 200 or fewer employees where training falls down.)

- **Too few sales calls on new prospects.** When a company is struggling, salespeople almost always do something that worsens the situation: they make fewer sales calls. It's easier to make a lot of sales calls when you've got an unblemished product (I think that's true, but I've never been in a position to sell such a product). When the product isn't the best, salespeople make fewer sales calls on their regular accounts and practically none on new prospects. The result is predictable: they become less effective on each sales call, because they put more pressure on themselves to make each call pay off bigger. They also have more time between sales calls to stew about the ones that got away. This automatically leads them back to "We need a better product to sell."

- **Not enough salespeople.** Larry Weinberg owned the Portland Trail Blazers for most of the eleven years I worked there. One time we were discussing our sponsorship sales staff. We had just hired our second salesperson. "What's next?" Larry asked.

"I'd like to hire a salesperson a year for twenty years and have each one make over $100,000 a year," I said.

"Say that again?"

I said it again.

"Would you care to explain that idea?" Larry asked.

"Well, I figure that an important part of my job is to create more sponsorship opportunities. More sponsorship opportunities will lead to more revenue. The more successful I am at that, the more salespeople we'll need to sell the stuff. The cost of our salespeople, including benefits, is about 6 percent of what they sell. If we do indeed add a salesperson a year for

twenty years and they're all making $100,000, you'll make a fortune."

Larry nodded his head and asked, "How about adding *two* salespeople a year for twenty years?"

I have consulted with a lot of teams and companies, and I haven't yet run into a situation where there were too many salespeople. I look at the number of salespeople the way McDonald's looks at the number of franchises. In the 1970s, McDonald's thought it had reached saturation in the United States with 1,000 stores. But they decided to expand. Expand they did — to 31,000 stores worldwide. Many companies think they've reached saturation in number of sales-people. What if these companies thought like McDonald's for a while? Simply: these companies would ramp up their revenues too.

If a salesperson costs 10 percent of the revenue he or she brings in, why not add more salespeople? And then add more to that?

What if the cost of sales rises to 15 percent of rev-enue, or more? That happened with the owner of a team in a new minor league. He said that the cost of sales was killing him. He came from a business in which cost of sales was less than 10 percent. In this new league, it was running about 25 percent. I told him I had a solution.

"What's that?" he asked.

"Fire all the salespeople."

He thought for a few seconds. "If I do that," he said, "I won't have *any* sales."

"But your cost of sales would be zero percent," I said. "Don't get caught up in cost of sales. Get caught up in revenue. So what if your first year costs you 25 percent? What's it cost to renew those sales? About 5 percent. Get caught up in revenue."

Massaging the Oilers

I started to poke the feet of the Edmonton Oilers.

The first thing one of the salespeople said to me was, "If we had a winning team, we could sell a lot more tickets."

I said, "And how about lowering the prices?"

The salesperson really brightened when I said that. "Yeah, that would really help. Our tickets are way over-priced."

That salesperson had just reiterated a fantasy of sales-people for generations: a perfect product at a ridiculously low price. That's a fantasy, however, that never comes true.

I had to wait a few minutes to talk to the Oilers' other salesperson. He was on the phone writing an order. After the phone call, I introduced myself. I then asked, "How do you get most of your orders?"

He pointed to the phone. "They call up."

The season ticket base had slid from 14,000 to 5,500. Obviously not enough people called up.

So let's see how the sales staff measured up to my poking their feet:

- Low morale.

- Inadequate training.

- Too few sales calls on new prospects.

- Not enough salespeople.

I had planned to spend two days up in Edmonton read-ing signs. Instead, I spent just one day. Reading the signs was that easy. At the end of the day, I met with Peter Pocklington.

"Well," he said, "do we have a chance?"

"Yes," I replied. "This can be turned around. You won't have to move the team to the United States. But you have to do two things. One of them you won't be able to do."

"What are the two things?" he asked.

"First, you're going to have to pay my company a fortune for six months."

He asked me how much a fortune was.

I told him.

He said, "I can do that."

I said, "I know that. That's the one you can do. The other one you can't do."

"What's that?"

"You can't talk to the media for six months."

Peter sat at his desk, thinking. This was a tough request. You see, Peter thought he was smart enough to convince the media that he was a terrific team owner.

He talked to the media regularly. They whacked him regularly and often in the newspapers, television, and radio. That just strengthened his resolve. He would try harder. The media would listen, then whack him again, harder.

After thinking for a minute, Peter said, "I can do the second thing. I can go to Maui for a couple of months to ease into it."

I thought maybe Maui was the rehab center for getting away from the press. I told him to see Gene Clark.

I had my doubts, but sure enough, Peter gagged himself for six months. We were off to the races to save the team for Edmonton.

We started with the ticket sales staff. Here's what we did:

- **Increased the sales staff.** We went from two sales-people to fifteen. That's right, fifteen. In little Edmonton, Alberta, Canada.

- **Injected enthusiasm into the sales staff.** We gave them something popular to sell. The team wasn't getting any better; they wouldn't make the playoffs. But we developed a ticket plan that was very popular.

  The plan had always been there; we just formalized it. Unlike most teams, many of the Oilers' season tickets were owned not by corporations, but by the fans. Most of the time, these fans had partners who shared the tickets and the costs. As prices rose, they had to find more people to share with. When they couldn't find another partner, they stopped buying tickets. They loved hockey, but they couldn't afford the whole package.

Our solution was simple. We marketed pre-selected ticket packages that together equaled a full season ticket. In other words, we found the extra partners they needed to share the cost of season tickets. Every hockey fan in Edmonton could afford to go to the games. Our sales staff were overjoyed. Armed with these new ticket packages, they invaded the corporations.

- **Improved training.** The Oilers' ticket salespeople, both of them, were self-trained — you know, try something and see if it works. That might have been okay had they tried a lot more things and made a lot more errors to lead them to something that worked. However, the sales staff kept trying the same thing and making the same error over and over.

  We now had fifteen salespeople, but we didn't need fifteen laboratories conducting trial and error experiments. So we trained the sales staff. Normally, when I go into a situation like this, I work with the people I'm given. I don't bring a battalion of people with me. In the Oilers' situation, however, we needed big results fast, so I brought in reinforcements.

  One reinforcement was young Dave Cohen, a student of mine when I taught at the University of Portland. I brought Dave in for a six-month stint as ticket sales manager. He would apply the experience he had gained selling tickets for minor-league teams in Quad Cities, Iowa, and Spokane, Washington. Then he could either stay with the Oilers or move on to a major-league team in the United States.

  My other recruit was Doug Piper, my partner in SRO Partners Inc., our sports marketing company at the time in Portland. He would be the project manager. While Dave lived full-time in Edmonton, Doug would fly in for a week or so per month.

- **Made more sales calls on new prospects.** Our fifteen salespeople focused mainly on new business. With our new staff trained and armed with some afford-able ticket packages, sales went from 5,500 season tickets to 13,000. To visualize the improvement, take a pen and a piece of paper. Position the tip of the pen in the lower left-hand corner of the paper. Now, draw a line to the upper right-hand corner. That's what happens when you expand the sales staff, train them, and go after new business.

    By increasing sales from 5,500 season tickets to 13,000, the Edmonton Oilers reached a magical tar-get. Why was it magical? The National Hockey League has a financial assistance package, amounting to sev-eral million American dollars, for Canadian teams because of the different values of the Canadian and American dollars. To receive the money, Canadian teams have to reach certain benchmarks — for the Oilers, 13,000 season tickets was one of them. So, in effect, the 13,000th season ticket was sold for several million dollars. How would you like to get the com-mission for that sale?

Keep the Feet Happy

This chapter may have seemed bor-ing to you. You might have been expecting some outrageous mar-keting idea. Outrageous feet?

Just thinking about the sales staff is outrageous at some companies. That was the case with the Edmonton Oilers. Like many other teams, the Oilers marketed themselves with an old-fashioned philosophy: "If you win, the fans will come." That may seem logical to a fan, but it's wrong. A better rule is

"If you win, the fans might come or they might not." Or to put this concept into general business language:

> If you have a great product, the buyers might buy
> and they might not.

The Oilers had the greatest product in the history of the National Hockey League, yet the number of season ticket renewals fell each time they won a championship. A lot of that was due to rising ticket prices, but if the Oilers had built and trained a sales staff the way we did, they could have kept themselves economically strong. Perhaps Peter Pocklington could have afforded to keep Wayne Gretzky. Perhaps they would still be winning championships.

Before I left the Edmonton Oilers, I said to Peter, "Peter, promise me one thing."

"Sure, what is it?"

"Promise me that you will never, ever not fully market again."

"I promise," he said.

"Even if you go back to winning championships."

"I promise never to not fully market again," he said.

Peter kept his promise until he sold the team a few years later.

A SIMPLE TEST YOU CAN TAKE

1. A sales staff is only as good as the product it sells. (True/False)

2. Our sales staff is big enough right now. (True/False)

3. Our salespeople are well trained. (True/False)

4. Our salespeople call on new prospects regularly and often. (True/False)

Answers

1. False, but true if you do one thing. A sales staff should do better when it is selling a better product. However, selling the best product in the NHL didn't help the Edmonton Oilers' sales staff. If the sales staff is fully trained, then the answer is true — the sales staff would do better selling a better product.

2. False. If you answered true, you're probably thinking about expense. Forget expense for the moment. Pretend salespeople are *free*. If salespeople are free, how many more would you need to maximize the revenues of your company? One? Ten? A hundred?

Let's say you said, "Two." What would it take to pay for those two salespeople? Write down this number in the margin of this page. Now, where could you find the money? No, no, don't slash your training budget, if you have one. Look to your advertising budget. Usually, you can take a small portion from that to pay for two salespeople. We did that at the New Jersey Nets. In the early 1990s, their ad budget was $200,000 — far less, they protested, than other NBA teams. I introduced them to the outrageous idea that we could slash the ad budget and yet be more effective (see chapter 11, "Don't Throw Your Money into a Tornado"). However, instead of just slashing the ad budget, we used the money to hire salespeople.

3. False. I'm going to assume that your sales staff isn't as well trained as it should be, because I see so few well-trained sales staffs when I visit teams or companies.

Sales training often gets placed near the bottom of the priority list. The sales manager is too busy, or outside training gets cut out of the budget. It happens in sports all the time. Typically, a team will build a $5 million training center for its athletes and hire specific skill coaches (like strength coaches or conditioning coaches) to try to create a better product. To help pay for the multimillion-dollar training center and its personnel, the team will do some budget cutting. One of the first things to go is training for the salespeople. This leaves only one way to maximize sales: create an outstanding team. And remember, even with a great team, sales may not reach their potential. Don't depend on your product to be your marketing genius.

4. False. I know this answer is false. Most sales staffs make calls to people they are comfortable with — current customers. Cold-call selling is brutal. It's hard to get an appointment. It's tough to make the sale. Heck, there's a lot of competition out there.

To maximize revenues from your sales staff, you have to do two things:

1. Get your regular customers to buy more.

2. Steal customers from your competition.

If your sales staff isn't consistently trying to get new customers, then the only way you can increase revenue is to get your regular customers to buy more. Getting a sales staff to go after new business, however, takes training. Let's hope training wasn't a victim of your last budget cut.

CHAPTER 6

Hit 'Em Where They Ain't

When I was thirteen, a boy in suburban Detroit, I had a newspaper route. I delivered fifty papers every day. It took me about an hour. However, at least half the houses I passed didn't subscribe to my paper.

It took me a few months to figure it out. If I could turn these folks into paying customers, it wouldn't take much more time to deliver the paper to twice as many people. I began to think: How can I get them to subscribe?

I did some research. I learned the names of the people who didn't subscribe, the people whose houses I rode by each day. I then wrote a letter and dropped it in their mailboxes. The letter went like this:

> I'm the paper boy for the *Detroit News*. You may have seen me. I ride my bike past your house at the same time every day, rain or shine. I could easily deliver a paper to you, just like I do to your neighbors.
>
> There's a lot of interesting articles in the paper, and I think you'll really enjoy the *Detroit News*.

If you'd like to try it, just hang the enclosed card on your doorknob, and I'll deliver the *News* for a week at my expense. If you like it, I'll just keep on delivering it. I collect once a month.

Within three months, I was delivering 100 newspapers in about the same time as it had taken me to deliver 50. I had effectively doubled my pay. A few months later, I tried the same letter on an adjoining neighborhood. Soon I had 150 subscribers, and it didn't take much more time. For a little extra effort, I was making three times as much.

Although I didn't know it, I had tiptoed into the world of marketing and direct response. And I had done something bold and audacious: I had given something away that I was supposed to sell. How could anybody make money doing that? It was outrageous. At the tender age of thirteen, I was already Marketing Outrageously.

What to Do When Nobody Believes You

Imagine yourself in this situation: Your competitors are huge, established global companies. They're big enough to have nuclear missiles. You're a little guy, just past the struggling start-up stage. If you poke your head out of your foxhole, they can push a button and obliterate you. These big-fisted competitors are General Motors, Toyota, Ford, Daimler-Benz, Honda, Nissan, and VW.

Even though this is a story about behemoth-type companies, and you may not play in a league that large, it's the *strategy* that is applicable to any size company.

The company facing these giants was Hyundai. When I think of Hyundai's history in the United States, I think of another imported car, the Yugo.

You may remember the Yugo jokes:

Q. *How do you double the value of your Yugo?*
A. Fill the gas tank.
Q. *How do you make a Yugo go faster?*
A. Use a tow truck.
Q. *What do you call a Yugo that breaks down after 100 miles?*
A. An overachiever.

Yugo and Hyundai started in the same era in the United States: 1982 for Yugo, 1986 for Hyundai. Both competed with each other in the sub-$6,000 low-price category; Yugo priced at $3,995, the Hyundai Excel at $5,195. Other competitors were the Chevrolet Chevette, the Dodge Colt, the Honda Civic, the Nissan Sentra, and the Toyota Tercel.

The Yugo and the Hyundai Excel were both poor quality vehicles. In the crummy car category, Yugo ran away with the honors; AAA's magazine *Via* ranked the Yugo as the worst car *ever* in the United States. The Yugo, of course, failed. The Hyundai Excel, unfortunately, ranked far closer to Yugo than it did to the Honda Civic and the Toyota Tercel. In fact, Hyundai started to gather its own set of jokes.

In its first two years in the U.S., Hyundai had terrific sales. Unfortunately, those terrific sales ultimately hurt them because the cars were poorly made, and they sold those poorly made cars to noncreditworthy customers (subprime loans, anybody?). When many of the cars were ultimately repossessed, the value of the relatively new clunker was less than the outstanding loans.

However, unlike Yugo, Hyundai eventually became emminently successful. What in the world could have been the difference?

It came down to one decision in 1998.

Hyundai had to make a choice: (1) abandon the United States as a market, or (2) compete like crazy.

They were losing tons of money in the U.S. That type of bleeding could not possibly continue. It would have been a good financial decision to leave the United States. Pull up and go home. Or, *compete.*

To compete Hyundai had to do two things:

1. Dramatically improve its quality.

2. Convince the American buyer that it had improved quality dramatically.

Both of these things could cost a fortune. Would that be like throwing good money after bad? A *lot* of good money after a lot of bad money.

Hyundai decided to compete. Improving quality was relatively easy. Heck, Hyundai had been making quality vehicles in Korea for years. It had chosen to enter the U.S. market with a cheap vehicle. To compete in the U.S., the company would have to install the quality that it already knew back home. Yes, it could upgrade the quality.

Convincing Americans that the Hyundai had improved quality was another matter. First of all, it would cost a for-tune for advertising. General Motors spent $3.1 billion in advertising back in 1998 and $4.01 billion in 1999. Try out-shouting them.

But, let's suppose that Hyundai budgeted a quasi-fortune. Then what would it say? Something like the following?

> "Hey, after producing crummy cars in the U.S., we have now decided to produce a quality car. Believe us, we're now producing quality cars. Quality, qual-ity, quality, that's us. Trust us."

Who in the world would believe that? Would you? I wouldn't.

Hyundai decided to put its money where its mouth was. The company answered that quality issue with one phrase: **"We guarantee your Hyundai car drivetrain for 10 years or 100,000 miles."**

At the time, General Motors and the other car companies were offering drivetrain warranties for three years and 50,000 miles. GM didn't have to offer anything more; remember they were spending *billions* telling us that they were the best.

With the increased quality backed up with a wonderful warranty, Hyundai made another big decision: they did *not* increase the price of their cars. In fact, they *added* additional benefits like leather seats without increasing the price of the car. The bargain-car shopper then found these attributes in a Hyundai:

1. **A low-priced car.** It was practically cheaper than anything out there.

2. **A low-priced car with some high price attributes.**

3. **A 10-year, 100,000-mile drivetrain warranty.** This warranty included a 5-year, 50,000-mile bumper-to-bumper warranty. So what if Hyundai's quality reputation wasn't pretty; if anything went wrong during that warranty time period, Hyundai would fix it for free. Good-bye repair bills. This warranty also included roadside assistance for five years.

It took a while for the quality to catch up with the marketing. Hyundai's quality didn't come overnight. In 2001, Hyundai ranked near the bottom in vehicle quality, judged by J. D. Powers — thirty-second out of thirty-seven cars ranked. In 2004, however, they ranked *seventh*. Then, in 2009,

Hyundai *surpassed Toyota* to fourth place, behind only Lexus, Porsche, and Cadillac.

And, as they were improving their product, they had *sales*. Lots of sales. In fact, they are now poised to surpass Dodge and Nissan in U.S. sales.

Hyundai has also sprung into the higher priced vehicles market. In 2009, the Hyundai Genesis ($32,250) was voted by journalists as the North American Car of the Year.

So, in just one decade, Hyundai went from almost leaving the U.S. to one of the fabulous success stories in the troubled automotive business. Yes, making the decision to create a quality car was the right decision. But that wasn't enough. Hyundai put its money where its mouth was with the 10-year 100,000-mile warranty, which was far greater than any of its competition's. This was clearly hitting them where they ain't.

THE ANT GOES TO WAR

This story may seem dated. Heck, it's about a company that started twenty-five years ago. It's about a teeny company going against giants. The teeny company won. They won because of a most outrageous marketing idea. This is the perfect example of Hitting 'Em Where They Ain't.

So, again, imagine yourself in this situation: Instead of cars this time, it's software. Your competitors are huge, established companies. Like Hyundai's competitors, these software companies also have nuclear missiles. You're a little guy, of course, just past the struggling start-up stage. Remember, don't poke your head out of your foxhole; it could be fatal.

That's what Steve Case, CEO of America Online, faced in the mid-'90s. His big-fisted competitors were Sears, IBM, and H&R Block.

So what did Case do? He pushed his own button. He unleashed the fury of 250 million AOL computer disks — one for almost every living human in the United States. With one of these disks, you could install AOL's software free, and you could connect to AOL for a month — also free.

Here's how you were carpet-bombed with disks:

- If you bought a computer magazine, you got one of AOL's free disks.

- If you got a free bag of peanuts on American Airlines, you got a free AOL disk.

- If you bought flash-frozen steaks from Omaha Steaks, you got a free AOL disk.

- If you went to an NFL game, you got a free AOL disk.

You've Got Mail

- If you just stayed home and looked in your mailbox, you got a free AOL disk.

You'd be hard pressed to find anybody who didn't get one of AOL's disks back then. If I had kept all the ones I got, I could have re-roofed my house with them.

When Steve Case pushed his marketing button, his giant competitors didn't see it coming. They didn't even consider him a competitor in the race to cyberspace. AOL was beneath their radar.

First, there was CompuServe, owned by H&R Block. CompuServe had been around since the early '80s and had grown 30 to 40 percent annually. It had about a million subscribers when Case pushed the button.

Next in line was Prodigy, owned by Sears, IBM, and Trintex, who had reached into their vaults and spent $500 million to launch its online service. Prodigy software was available at 500 Sears stores for $39.95. Monthly service was $9.95. Spending $20 million a year on advertising, Prodigy signed up 500,000 subscribers.

America Online had only 300,000 subscribers, $40 million annual revenue, and a need for more investors. Then Case pushed his marketing button, and AOL gained 70,000 new customers in January 1994 alone. By August it had signed on more than a million, and over the next few years, 23 million.

If you're curious about the *monthly* revenue from those 23 million subscribers, first remember AOL's annual revenue had been $40 million. Well, just a couple of years after Case pushed his Marketing Outrageously button, AOL's *monthly* revenue was $298 million — almost one-third of a billion dollars per month, from a company that wasn't even taken seriously by its competitors.

(The bad news was that in that first year AOL got more business than it could handle. Its marketing strategy was so successful it outstripped AOL's ability to provide the services it promised. Dialups generated busy signals and angry customers. The company became known as "America On Hold." You see, AOL was geared up to handle only 8,217 users at any one time. To fuel its growth, AOL certainly had to fix that, which it did. After all, AOL had all this new cash rolling in every month.)

Invisible Armor

CompuServe and Prodigy marketed themselves like Coca-Cola, Pizza Hut, and Chevy — TV commercials, magazine ads, billboards. And it worked. Both gained a lot of new subscribers every year. They didn't feel any need to market outrageously. Why be outrageous when you can grow safely and steadily?

Marketing Outrageously isn't really outrageous; it's just unusual. In many companies, however, even being unusual can pose a danger. Naysayers are always standing in the shadows, daggers at the ready. Try to picture this scenario at CompuServe or Prodigy when you're trying to bring up the concept of giving away their program *free*.

"You're saying we should *give away* our software?" says the naysayer executive.

"Yes," you say. "AOL gave away its software, and it's getting hundreds of thousands of subscribers."

"We charge $39.95 in 11,000 stores. That's synergy at its best. You want us to just toss that forty bucks in the trash?"

"We might lose the forty," you say, "but we'll get twenty a month from each subscriber, month after month. If we dramatically increase our number of subscriptions, we won't even miss the $39.95."

"We aren't AOL, we're a real company with real roots. We don't need to market outrageously."

"But it may be far more dangerous *not* to market outrageously."

The naysayer's eyes narrow. "What's your name again?"

However, if you have the guts to try Marketing Outrageously, there's an invisible armor you can put on to protect your back. It's called testing.

AOL decided to test its idea by measuring just one benchmark: If the disks were given away, how many people would use them to log on and become paying subscribers?

The initial test cost $250,000. AOL had its disks distributed as on-serts — enclosed with a computer magazine in a sealed plastic bag. The on-sert added value for the magazine (Free Computer Disk Inside!), and the magazine's audience was a natural target group. CompuServe and Prodigy advertised inside the same magazines, but AOL's on-sert totally preempted their ads.

AOL found that for every 100 disks it gave away, ten people became paying subscribers. With that kind of response, paying to distribute more and more disks was easy. AOL began to use on-serts every month in computer magazines. I think I first tried AOL on my sixth free disk.

Then AOL went wild and began to distribute disks everywhere. If the on-sert worked in computer magazines, why not with airline peanuts? Frozen supermarket steaks? Local newspapers? As AOL sent out more and more disks with peanuts and steaks and whatever, its conversion percentage went down, but the number of subscribers went up and up and up. A million here, a million there — pretty soon you're Godzilla.

Are They Nuts?

If you'd been working at CompuServe or Prodigy when AOL launched its 250 million disk bombardment, you'd have figured AOL had gone stark raving crazy. After all, fewer than 10 percent of the people who got them would ever use them. Most people threw them away immediately. Such a waste! Why not just market your services the tried-and-true way and get the 30 percent annual increases? Heck, just going from 300,000 to 400,000 subscribers should have been good enough reason for AOL to break out the champagne. Instead, AOL blitzed the market outrageously.

AOL didn't sell the *concept* of online, it sold "try it now." CompuServe and Prodigy spent fortunes trying to persuade you to buy software so you could spend still more money using their services. AOL didn't try to educate; it just piqued your curiosity. Go ahead, just stick that free AOL disk into your computer and try it. We'll give you free e-mail. We'll even give you the first month's usage for free. Or you can go to a computer store and buy a competitor's program for $39.95. Thirty-nine-ninety-five or free, which will you take?

If AOL had modeled its marketing after CompuServe and Prodigy, here's what probably would have happened:

- **AOL would have helped expand the market.**
  CompuServe and Prodigy were using television commercials and magazine ads to promote the benefits of online services. AOL
  would have been just
  another voice in the choir.
  The formula is simple: More
  voices = more persuasion =
  more people thinking about
  online = a small portion of
  the consumers choosing
  which service they would
  like to subscribe to. AOL
  would have received its fair share of the expanding market, but CompuServe and Prodigy would have received their fair share also — and their fair share was a lot bigger than AOL's. So if AOL had chosen traditional marketing, it would have helped the market leaders grow stronger. Eventually, the market leaders would have turned that new strength on AOL.

- **AOL would still be number three — or out of business.** According to Jack Welch, chairman of General Electric, it's not good to be number three in a market, especially if number one and number two are giants. If a giant decides it wants your market share, you can quickly become insignificant or extinct.

Here's what happened because AOL marketed outrageously:

The online market didn't just expand, it exploded.

- **AOL quickly took the lion's share of the market.** It got almost all the new customers and, as its subscriber base grew, freely stole subscribers from its competitors. AOL eventually absorbed CompuServe, and Prodigy disappeared in a merger. Just a few years later, AOL merged with Time Warner, the parent of *Time* magazine, *Sports Illustrated,* and Warner Brothers, thus creating the world's largest media company. It was called a 'merger of equals,' and maybe it was, but I think they might have been referring to the amount of blood on the floor after the merger. Some folks, like Steve Case, walked away with billions. Others crawled away with millions. All that blood and all that walk-away money sometimes obscures the outrageous marketing that AOL did to even put themselves in that position.

Hit 'Em Where They Ain't

In the late 1890s, there was a major-league baseball player named Willie Keeler who could really hit 'em. A newspaper reporter asked him how he kept his batting average so high. Willie answered, "I hit 'em where they ain't."

When you think about it, that's not a bad philosophy for marketers. Hit 'em where your competition ain't. Or more to the point: Hit 'em where they ain't strong.

A SIMPLE TEST YOU CAN TAKE

1. Somewhere inside your product or company there's an outrageous marketing idea that could have a huge impact. What is that idea?

_____

_____

_____

2. What are the reasons you can't test that outrageous marketing idea?

a. _____

b. _____

c. _____

3. What is the reason you *can* test that outrageous marketing idea?

_____

_____

_____

4. Let's say you were CompuServe or Prodigy when AOL sprung its disk blitzkrieg. What would you have done?
   a. Run more ads in computer magazines.
   b. Run more ads on television.
   c. Stayed late and run off 100 copies of your résumé on the copying machine.
   d. Made a big effort to think outside the box.

Answers

1. If you work for a big company or one that's not struggling, it's harder to come up with outside-the-box marketing ideas. The reason? Perceived risk. In a big company, you may have to get approval from several levels of naysayers. And there are others, with daggers, just waiting for your idea to flop.

If you work for a smaller company or one that's not struggling, the attitude may be "If it ain't broke, don't fix it." Outside-the-box thinking says, "If it ain't broke, it will be, sooner or later. Why not upgrade now?" However, if you're with a small, struggling company, thinking outside the box is not optional. You have to do it to survive.

To come up with the right answer, always imagine yourself in a small, struggling company. What outside-the-box idea would really help you jump-start your company? Once you have a hint of an idea, write it down and follow the instructions in chapter 3, "Pushing the Outrageous Envelope."

2. Go ahead, write down your specific reasons for not testing an outrageous marketing idea. As many as you want. I'll wait.

Lack of money might be one reason.

If that's the case, make the test smaller. For instance, suppose AOL could not have afforded its $250,000 on-sert test. I'm sure it could have gotten a computer magazine to agree to a $25,000 test, which would have yielded the same answer: "We have to put all our resources into getting program disks into the hands of computer users."

Another reason for not testing might be that the idea really seems stupid. Nevertheless, if you think or feel that a stupid idea might work, go ahead and test it.

3. If you wrote something like "We might be able to dramatically increase our sales," then score yourself correct. That's reason enough.

4. d. Make a big effort to think outside the box. Your company may never use outside-the-box ideas, but that should not stop you from thinking that way. If nothing else, think about the competition. If you can show how a competitor might take big bites out of your market share, you might find your company more receptive to outside-the-box ideas.

Burger Battles

The folks at McDonald's declined to buy a sponsorship from me while I was with the Portland Trail Blazers. It wasn't the last time they turned me down. They gave me the bum's rush the first time I called on them as president of the New Jersey Nets.

The regional manager of McDonald's had agreed to see me. I had a neat promotional idea I thought would sell them a lot of burgers. But before I could get into my presentation, the manager said, "The only reason I agreed to see you was so you could read my lips."

Uh-oh, I thought, the read-my-lips line is usually not a good buying signal.

"I wanted you to know," he said slowly, "that McDonald's will never be associated with the New Jersey Nets. Never. Ever. Never-ever-ever. Never. You're a lousy team. You've got lousy owners. You've got lousy management. We won't allow our name to be associated with your team. Good-bye."

I packed up my briefcase and departed.

When I got outside, I stood by their front door and thought, "Who in the world can I get for this great promotion where we won't bring down their image and identity?"

I thought for a few seconds. Then the answer came to me. White Castle! White Castle was the first fast-food restaurant in the world, but it hadn't parlayed itself into a larger national or international chain like McDonald's, Burger King, or Wendy's. It was a down-home, blue-collar eatery all the way.

(I love White Castle burgers. They're small, greasy burgers, slathered with onions, that you buy by the bag, six for a couple of bucks. If you aren't born to the taste, I think it's difficult to develop a liking for them. In fact, my wife wouldn't even go into a White Castle after the first visit — she didn't like the smell. All those onions, probably.)

I made an appointment with White Castle and hoped I wouldn't get another lesson in lip reading. I took them the idea I had wanted to present to McDonald's. They loved it. The idea was the "family ticket package" — four $20 tickets to a Nets game, four meals at White Castle, a Nets cap, and a basketball, for only $39.95.

White Castle paid us about $150,000 for the radio sponsorship, which included this promotion. We would feature one game per month as the 'White Castle game.' We didn't expect White Castle to give us the hamburgers for free. After all, that was their business — they sold burgers. We paid them their retail price for the four meals, about $10 per package.

We sold tens of thousands of packages. In fact, the top three revenue days by an individual restaurant in White Castle's sixty-year history came from our family ticket promotion. The regional manager said that White Castle was going to build a statue of me at the home office in Columbus, Ohio.

A year later, I got a call from the regional marketing manager of McDonald's.

"Hey, Jon, buddy pal," he said (he must have had a convenient memory). He asked me to come out and see him. I agreed.

When I arrived at his office, there was none of this read-my-lips stuff. He said, "I want that White Castle promotion."

"Can't have it," I said. "White Castle signed a three-year deal. But I can put you in line."

"What do you mean?"

"Well, if you buy a sponsorship right now, I'll give you first rights to the promotion if White Castle chooses not to renew."

"How much are you talking about?" he asked.

"We've got a signage package that sells for $240,000."

"And that would include the first option on the White Castle promotion?"

I nodded my head.

We had a deal.

Two years later, I had left the Nets. My successor wanted to do a deal with McDonald's. More prestigious company, you know. He upped the price of the White Castle package so high that White Castle could no longer afford it. McDonald's exercised its option.

It has worked well for McDonald's in New Jersey.

I took the idea with me when I went to consult for the Sacramento Kings. There are no White Castles in Sacramento, so we presented the promotion to the McDonald's regional marketing manager in Sacramento.

"Does this promotion really work?" he asked me.

"Call your counterpart in New Jersey," I said. "He stood in line for three years to get this promotion."

CHAPTER 7

Horse of Opportunity

Centuries ago, opportunity was sometimes envisioned as a horse with wings. This wasn't one of those trained horses that kneeled down so you can easily get on it; this winged horse was always flying, zipping past. Sometimes it would appear out of nowhere when you needed it most — in the middle of a battle, perhaps. But you had to be alert and bold and quick; if you let it slip by, the opportunity to save yourself was gone.

I read about this Horse of Opportunity years ago in a magazine in some waiting room. As I sat reading, I thought about that winged horse. Picture it: The horse approaches; you trot alongside, grab the horse's wing, get a firm grip, and jump on. No sweat. Cowboys do it all the time in the movies (except for the wing). But if you don't see the Horse of Opportunity coming, or if you wait too long to decide, it slides swiftly by, and all you can do is grab for its slippery tail.

This Horse of Opportunity can represent a lot of different things — a job, a person, money, even peace of mind. But I've come to think of the Horse of Opportunity in terms of marketing.

Grab the wing of a flying horse? Sounds tricky, doesn't it? It's not. Here's why. First, you see the horse coming. When you see the horse, you can prepare to grab the wing. When you're prepared, all that's left to do is grab when the horse flies by.

How do you prepare? The first step is to understand that, in marketing, there really is a Horse of Opportunity. Once you've taken that step, you'll be amazed at how many Horses of Opportunity you see out there.

Unfortunately, many people never see the horse coming. Or they see it but don't prepare for it. Or they just feel it swish by, then look around as the horse is flying quickly away and say, "There goes that damn horse again." Usually, however, they're afraid to jump on it and hold on, not knowing where the Horse of Opportunity will take them.

I've been fortunate. I've seen the horse coming and grabbed the wings, more than once. I've had some wonderful rides and gone to some terrific places on the Horse of Opportunity. I highly recommend it. Try it. You'll have the ride of your life.

Method in the Madness

This chapter is about "Rare Opportunity." Sometimes this Rare Opportunity is given to you for free by your competitors. See how Southwest Airlines handled it later in this chapter.

Other times, the market just hands it to you. Lays it right out there on a platter where almost anybody can grab it.

The questions then become:

1. **Do you see this Rare Opportunity in time to do something about it?** Don't feel bad, most folks don't. However, since you're reading this book, my feeling is that your personal antenna is calibrated to sense Rare Big Opportunities most of the time.

2. **If you do see it, are you prepared to pounce on it?** This is a little more difficult to answer. This takes the effort to rally up the troops. But, again, you're reading this book, and your troops are probably used to you rallying them up.

3. **Do you have the guts?** You know there's going to be a slew of naysayers out there. Probably some pretty important naysayers. They can routinely make a case as to why the Rare Big Opportunity will fail and it will be the end of the world as we know it. So, that takes us back to #1 and #2. If you *see* the opportunity, just know that other folks won't, especially the naysayers. You'll have to paint a very vivid picture. The painting can't be modern art; in fact it's almost like painting by numbers. You know, plain and simple and understandable.

Sometimes Competitors Just Hand You the Rare Opportunity

If you could increase your revenue by 1.5 percent, but it would anger almost every one of your customers, would you do it? That's right, *anger* almost every one of your customers for 1.5 percent increase in revenue.

That's what the airlines did when they began charging for checked luggage.

Forget that the airlines don't give you food anymore. And that some charge for soft drinks. Or that they squeeze in a couple more rows of seats making everybody over five feet tall miserable for the entire flight. Forget all that stuff. The thing that fired up almost everybody was charging for checked luggage. (By the way, if the checked luggage didn't make it to the destination, you still paid to have it delivered someplace else.)

So, what's an easy way to differentiate yourself from an industry that seems to pride itself on angering its customers — and take advantage of this opportunity?

Easy, eh? Don't charge for checked luggage. We all know who figured that out. Southwest Airlines. Southwest is the one airline that doesn't follow the followers. It follows its own path. It doesn't make stupid mistakes. But let's hear from a naysayer.

Naysayer: By not charging for luggage, you're giving up 1.5 percent of your revenue. You're giving up a perfectly good way to gouge your customers and really anger them.

Southwest: Yeah, we're giving up that so-called revenue. But Dave Ridley, Southwest's senior vice president of marketing and revenue management, credited the "bags fly free" campaign for increasing their revenue by one billion dollars in the first year after it was launched.

Was this point of differentiation difficult to do for Southwest? Of course not. It wasn't charging for checked luggage in the first place. And when most of the other airlines decided to gouge, it gave Southwest the perfect opportunity to again differentiate itself and jump on that opportunity. All Southwest had to do was use its regular ad budget to tell us folks.

The Weird Tie-In Can Be the Rare Opportunity

There are some ideas that come along that at first blush (or second or third) just seem too outrageous to even consider. However, if an idea doesn't make you laugh or at least flinch, then the idea probably isn't going to be a great one.

Aflac and the duck is one example (see chapter 3). Probably a lot of initial flinching on that one.

How about this one? Onions for kids. It's not difficult to market things that kids like, like bananas or strawberries or blueberries. But onions? C'mon, that's crazy.

Let's bring in a secret weapon to help.

In this case, the secret weapon is Shrek. That's right Shrek and onions for kids.

Shrek, of course, is an animated green ogre who has lots of adventures after leaving his peaceful life in a swamp. As of 2010, there have been four *Shrek* movies by Dreamworks. Each movie has been wildly successful, making Dreamworks a worthy competitor to Pixar in the area of computer animated feature films.

Shrek also has had large endorsement deals that range from companies like Hewlett-Packard to Bank of America.

Then along came onions, the Vidalia Onion Committee to be precise. It is an association of 100 growers of Vidalia, a trademarked sweet onion that is grown in southeastern Georgia.

The onion folks used Shrek in just three ways: (1) on their packages, (2) in their store displays, and (3) on their website. No national TV ads, no local TV or radio ads, no ad push.

Dreamworks Animation SKG, Inc. gave Vidalia the rights to use Shrek for about $300,000 in publicity and marketing, which included the costs of packaging, store placards, and bags. The packaging and point-of-sale material was all the stuff that Vidalia needed to put the brakes on shopping carts with kids riding inside as they came to the display.

How successful was Shrek?

Well, Vidalia could have expected a *drop* in sales because excessive rain and cold had delayed the harvest by two weeks. With Shrek, however, they experienced a 35 percent *increase* in medium-size Vidalias, the bag size that featured Shrek.

Your Opportunity Is Staring at You

You'll have the opportunity, you know. It might not be something big. It might be something that your competitors just hand you on a platter. But somewhere, sometime, you'll find yourself looking the Horse of Opportunity straight in the eye. It will come in fast, and, unfortunately, you won't have time to take a test drive. It's go for it — grab the wings and hoist yourself up — or sit there and watch a great and rare opportunity fly by. There's no consolation in waving to it as it gallops past.

A SIMPLE TEST YOU CAN TAKE

1. Have you seen the Horse of Opportunity before and not jumped on? If so, what was the opportunity?

_____

_____

_____

_____

_____

2. When you missed that opportunity, what results did you not get?

_____

_____

_____

_____

3. I'm going to be looking for the Horse of Opportunity in the future. (True/False)

4. I'm going to jump on that Horse of Opportunity the next time I see it and let it take me for a wild and wonderful ride. (True/False/Don't know)

Answers

1. Don't be embarrassed to write about a missed opportunity. Heck, I've thought about writing a book about people who didn't even see the Horse of Opportunity coming, but there would be so many examples I wouldn't know where to start. For instance:

Two young guys started a pizza kitchen near the University of Michigan. They couldn't afford a space big enough for a sit-down restaurant, so they used their beat-up Volkswagen to deliver pizzas to the dorms.

The business didn't prosper, so the two partners sat down to discuss the situation. They decided the business would never support them both. One partner said, "I'll leave and give you my 50 percent of the business. But I want the Beetle."

Tom Monaghan, the other partner, saw the Horse of Opportunity. He agreed to the deal.

Monaghan went on to build Domino's Pizza, which practically invented the home-delivery pizza business. He accumulated a net worth of over $1 billion. The other partner got the beat-up VW.

So don't feel bad about missing the Horse of Opportunity. Just knowing that you missed it makes you more likely to see it coming next time.

2. Sure, this may seem cruel, making you quantify what you missed. It's like ask-

ing Tom Monaghan's partner to write "$1,000,000,000" in that space. But do it anyway. Quantify it. You're training yourself to see the Horse of Opportunity the next time it comes flying into view.

3. If you answered the first two questions of this simple test, your answer to this question will be True, whether you marked that answer or not. Why? Because you will be looking, at least subconsciously, for that Horse of Opportunity.

4. I'm not sure how you answered this, but I hope the answer wasn't False. If you answered True or Don't know, then at least you're aware that the Horse of Opportunity is out there. The Horse will come toward you, and as it approaches, you'll have to decide quickly whether or not to jump on. If you answered True or Don't know, I believe you'll ride.

CHAPTER 8

New as a Way of Life

When I was an adjunct professor teaching marketing, I made only one book required reading. I could give you 1,000 tries and you wouldn't guess. It was *Veeck as in Wreck,* by Bill Veeck.

Bill Veeck was a pioneer in outrageous sports marketing. He's best remembered for the time he sent in a midget as a leadoff batter when he owned the St. Louis Browns in the 1950s. He also invented the exploding scoreboard, fireworks nights, and anything that would please the fans. Most of the whacko stuff you see in sports started with Bill Veeck.

Every few years, I make it a point to read *Veeck as in Wreck* all over again. I come up with new, outrageous ideas each time I do. Once, when I was vice president for marketing for the hapless Buffalo Braves, I was reading again about the midget, and an outrageous idea struck me. Midgets wouldn't be much help on a basketball team, of course, but maybe the opposite would. I remembered reading that the tallest man in the world lived in Brazil. He was nine-feet-three-inches tall. Why not pull a reverse midget stunt?

I mentioned this to our coach, Cotton Fitzsimmons. All we'd have to do, I said, is bring him into one game — just like Veeck's midget. To my surprise, Cotton thought it might be fun. After all, we were a lousy team, destined to move away from Buffalo, so why not do something outrageous before we left?

I immediately got on the phone and started tracking down this giant.

The next day, Cotton came into my office. "Can that nine-foot-three guy run?" he asked.

I said I didn't know, but probably not. He'd have to walk out to center court for the jump, then we'd have to call time-out to let him walk out of the game.

A couple of days passed. Cotton came into my office again. "You know, maybe we could get our fitness guy to work with him. Maybe we could get him to trot," Cotton said.

Cotton was now thinking that this guy might come in at the end of a close game — if we ever had one — and just stand there waving his arms as his opponent tried to pass the ball inbounds. "That would be like throwing the ball over a mountain. Heck, he'd be our one-play-a-game specialist."

Two days later, I got the word about the giant. What I had missed reading a few weeks before was that the tallest man in the history of the world had died.

That didn't stop Cotton. "Maybe he's got a brother. Or even a sister."

I still read *Veeck as in Wreck* every few years. Veeck was an outrageous thinker for his time, and if he were alive today, you know what? He'd still be outrageous.

Another outrageous owner was Charlie O. Finley of the Oakland Athletics. Ponder this for a moment: Charlie designated a mule as the team mascot. He named it Charlie O, after himself.

Charlie Finley put color into baseball. The Athletics were the first team to wear white shoes — at the time, outrageous. Before Finley, baseball shoes came in the same colors as Henry Ford's Model T: any color you wanted, as long as it was black.

Before Finley dressed his players in green jerseys, baseball teams wore white jerseys at home and gray on the road.

Finley also petitioned Major League Baseball to change the color of baseballs to orange.

Just about the time he was making these color changes, I was a young entrepreneur in Chicago. One day I got a surprise phone call from Charlie O — the man, not the mule. I didn't know him, but a friend of his knew me and told him we should get together.

I went over to his posh Chicago apartment on Lake Michigan. We chatted a few minutes. Then he said he wanted to show me something. "Wait right there," he said as he left the room.

A minute or so later he came back with a box. What could he have in there? Some wild new baseball idea? He opened it up.

It was hair. Or, as he said, "Store-bought hair." Charlie O was bald.

He lifted the white hair out of the box and for fifteen minutes showed me all the tricks he used to make the thing look real. Then he said he had to run. We walked out together into the winter chill of Chicago.

That was the last I heard from Charlie. But every once in a while I'll remember one of Charlie's outrageous ideas, and I'll think: Can I make that work today?

Recently I did that. I made one of his ideas work for me. Not the store-bought hair, but the orange baseball. We used a day-glo orange baseball with one of Mandalay's minor-league baseball teams. We did it to signal change.

Charlie O would be proud. The man, not the mule.

A MATTER OF SURVIVAL

"What's new?"

You've probably asked somebody that, or been asked it. It's a mundane question, like "How ya doin'?" The usual answer is "Not much." Or maybe "Nuthin'."

But the next time you get asked, "What's new," you should silently answer, "A lot, and if you've got a day and a half, I'll tell you." Here's why.

I always enjoy having dinner with Kunitake Ando, a friend of mine from Tokyo, who was for ten years the president of Sony/USA. When I got to know him, he was Sony's president and chief operating officer. Mr. Ando knew what Sony scientists were dreaming up and frequently gave me a glimpse of the near future. It was usually something I would never have dreamed of at the time. Like the three-pound laptop as powerful as a fully equipped desktop (I was lugging around a nine-pound rock then) that six months later was launched as the Sony Vaio.

I once said to him, "It must be frightening, having to come up with new ideas all the time for products that might have a life cycle of six months."

Ando laughed and said, "New is a way of life with us. A way of life! If we don't create new things all the time, we die in the marketplace."

I said, "Wow, can I write that down?" Ando nodded.

I wrote it down as it applied to me in marketing: New as a way of life; if we don't do *marketing* things, we'll get beat in the marketplace.

The flight back from Tokyo to New York took about fifteen hours. For almost every minute of that flight I was thinking, "New as a way of life; if we don't do new, we perish in the marketplace."

Follow That Engineer!

Marketing people aren't on the same treadmill that the Sony engineers are on — the invent-a-new-product-in-six-months-or-die treadmill. But it's not a bad idea for marketers to look at the product people as role models — without the dying part, of course. Instead of inventing a new product every six months, the marketer should invent new ways to market his or her product every six months.

Skeptical marketers might say inventing new ways to market their products (1) takes too much time, (2) is unnecessary because their marketing efforts are adequate, or (3) is impossible, because there's nothing new under the sun about marketing their products. The answers to those objections:

1. It doesn't take much time at all.

2. Their marketing efforts may seem adequate now, but might not be in six months.

3. There are lots of new ways to market any product.

Marketers can and should think like those Sony engineers. Here's a new mantra marketers should adopt:

> New is a way of life with us marketers. A way of life! If we don't create new ways to market things all the time, we die in the marketplace.

Need an example? Let's go to the movies. You've seen formula movies. Many of the John Wayne movies followed a formula: good guy, bad guy, good guy wins at the end. The *Rocky* movies fit this formula as if it were created for them. Well, movie marketing usually follows a recipe, too:

- **One part heavy TV advertising.** Start the television advertising a few weeks before the movie is first shown in theaters; continue for the first week or three after it debuts. If a movie costs $60 million to $80 million, advertise more heavily.

- **One part newspaper ads.** When the movie debuts, run big ads. As the movie plays, let the ads shrink.

- **One part public relations.** Get the stars on the talk-show circuit.

This movie-marketing formula is even more entrenched than the Hollywood plot formula. Marketing costs for a typical movie: about $30 million.

And then along came Artisan Entertainment's *The Blair Witch Project.*

Artisan tossed out all three parts of the standard marketing formula. No TV advertising. No big newspaper ads. No stars appearing on talk shows. Instead of using the old formula, they came up with New as a Way of Life.

Here's the new marketing formula Artisan invented for *The Blair Witch Project:*

- **Community trendsetters.** Artisan hired about 100 college interns and sent them to clubs, bookstores, hip clothing stores, coffee shops — wherever young people hung out — to distribute missing-person fliers. To get the full story about the three "missing" people, you were directed to the *Blair Witch* website.

- **Website.** The *Blair Witch* website looked like it was about actual events, not a movie. It was easy to believe three college kids had disappeared while looking for a witch and that the video footage they shot had been found. Visitors to the site spread the word to bulletin boards and chat rooms, and the website got 115 million hits. In essence, the audience did the marketing for Artisan.

- **No stars promoting the film.** The three stars of the movie didn't make the talk-show circuit. This added to the authenticity. After all, if you bought into the website, these three stars were probably dead — so how could they go on *Good Morning America* or *Jay Leno?*

- **Sold-out theaters.** *The Blair Witch Project* opened at only twenty-seven theaters in major markets. Each sold out. The following week, Artisan could have broadened the distribution to more than 2,000 theaters. They chose not to; they wanted to keep the "sold out" mentality. They limited the spread to 1,000 theaters.

The Blair Witch Project cost less than $50,000 to make, yet this glorified home movie grossed over $140 million in the United States and almost another $100 million internationally to bring the total to a quarter of a *billion* dollars in sales. Did it get those huge returns because it was the greatest movie since *Gone with the Wind?* I don't think so. I think it was because Artisan threw out the old marketing formula for movies and created its own.

Was every part of Artisan's marketing strategy new? Of course not. Hip-hop music labels use the "community trend-setters" strategy, and now every movie has its own website. Moreover, some movies can't get their stars on the talk-show circuit. What Artisan did was step away from the standard movie-marketing formula and create a formula that worked precisely and astoundingly well for a little movie called *The Blair Witch Project.*

Engineering Outrageous Sales

If the Sony engineers could keep coming up with new products time after time, I figured I could do that as a sports marketer. One way would be to invent new ways to sell tickets.

Most teams have just three ways to market tickets:

1. **Sales staff.** Ticket salespeople are generally telemarketers who call up everybody they know trying to sell season tickets and answer incoming calls for orders.

2. **Group ticket sales.** The same sales staff will sometimes call on churches and schools to sell tickets to groups.

3. **Box office.** Box office people sell tickets to the walk-up buyers.

When I joined the New Jersey Nets, I resolved to expand ticket sales by adding at least one new sales method every six months. This was more than a vague desire — it was absolutely necessary for our survival, as it was for those Sony engineers.

Here are some ideas we thought up that other teams weren't using:

1. **Direct-response ads.** Most sports teams used their ad money to (a) create an identity and (b) tell walk-up fans — on the day of the game — that there was a game that day. At the Nets, we marched to a different drummer: we ran nothing but direct-response ads. Our sole

measuring stick was how many tickets we sold in response to each ad. We measured the results precisely.

2. **Infomercials.** Teams with big budgets ran lots of thirty-second television commercials to build identity. We became the first team to run thirty-minute infomercials urging the viewer to pick up the phone *right now* and buy a ticket package.

3. **Ticket catalog.** Most sports teams printed up brochures to promote ticket packages, but left them at the box office. At the Nets, we printed a colorful, interesting ticket catalog. Our catalog resembled a slimmed-down Lands' End catalog, but instead of sweaters and shirts and ties, we featured a different ticket package on each page. You can buy lots of mailing lists, but I had never seen a list of "Nets fans," so we built our own 70,000-name database.

4. **Group ticket catalog.** Based on our success with the catalog, we promoted ticket packages to groups. We built a database of groups, such as teachers and classes raising money for extracurricular projects, that might buy discounted tickets and sell them at full price. We created a new catalog of ticket packages designed for groups, mailed it to our database addresses, and tripled our group sales.

5. **The Internet.** Before Amazon.com, before E*TRADE, before eBay, we didn't know much about the Internet, but neither did anyone else. We figured we might as well learn. We wanted New; the Internet was New.

A "New" Report Card

I'd love to be able to report that all of our new stuff worked out perfectly. But, of course, not all of it did. If we had given ourselves a report card, it would have looked like this:

New action	Grade	Comments
Direct-response ads	A	For every dollar we spent in advertising, we got $5 back — a terrific ratio for newspaper ads.
Infomercials	C	We ran our infomercial sporadically for five months and got a $3-to-$1 ratio. This wasn't bad, but so many companies were running infomercials that we couldn't buy as much TV time as we wanted.
Ticket catalog	A+	For every dollar we spent creating and mailing the catalog, we got $10.
Group ticket catalog	A+	We increased group ticket sales from $500,000 to $1.5 million, at a return far greater than $10-to-$1.
The Internet	I	Incomplete. The cost to create a website in 1995 was $100,000. That was too rich for us. As months went by, the cost went down, but then the NBA set up a website that included all its teams.
Final grade	A+	

Hold on, you say. How in the world could we get an A+ overall when our report card showed a C and an Incomplete?

We got an A+ because the things that worked, worked big. Our ticket catalog represented about 20 percent of our total ticket sales. Our group ticket catalog brought us an additional $1 million in revenue. And the things that didn't work didn't cost much to try.

New Doesn't Mean Huge

Okay, maybe these ideas weren't as big as AOL's diskette bombardment and maybe they were old stuff to other industries, but they were New as a Way of Life for us, and they paid off outrageously well. We accomplished several objectives:

1. **Increasing revenue.** If you ever make a list of why you should adopt New as a Way of Life, increasing revenue has to be at the top. We did that, at least with some of our new ideas.

2. **Getting rid of the same-old same-old.** The same-old same-old wasn't working. We kept the things that were working moderately well, improved them, and added some exciting new ideas. Eventually, this combination of improvement and innovation created a new corporate culture.

3. **Increasing staff enthusiasm.** Looking for ways to increase staff enthusiasm? A summer picnic isn't it. An across-the-board pay raise isn't it either. Both will work for the short term, but New as a Way of Life works best.

However, let me give you a word of warning. If you start New as a Way of Life, you'll encounter resistance from many of your staff. Why? Because it's new. The results are unknown. It might be successful, it might be a *failure.* (I emphasize "failure" because the fear of failure is greater than the hope for success.) And what happens when a new project fails? People get tarred and feathered. They get fired. Sometimes they get tarred and feathered and *then* fired. It's safer to do the same-old same-old, even if it isn't working very well. At least it's predictable. Nobody gets blamed, nobody gets fired — unless, of course, it drives the company into oblivion.

When adopting New as a Way of Life, it's better to keep it to yourself at first. If you make a big announcement about New as a Way of Life, you'll just set off alarms and send people screaming down the hallways and into the streets. Start a new project as if it's an experiment, not a wholesale change in philosophy. An experiment is considered temporary; if it's successful, everybody feels safe and buys in. After a few months, introduce another new project — another experiment. A few months later, yet another.

In time, the staff will embrace New as a Way of Life. Many will grow enthusiastic about creating new things from scratch that work. They'll start to expect new things; no more same-old same-old for them. New as a Way of Life will quickly become the corporate culture — without a decree, without a mandate, just naturally, one experiment at a time.

When you start thinking New as a Way of Life like a Sony engineer, you don't have to go out and buy a plastic shirt-pocket protector or start wearing thick-soled shoes. The only thing you have to do is think:

"New is a way of life with us. A way of life! If we don't create new ways to market things all the time, we die in the marketplace."

The Internet Can Fool You

New as a way of life has to include the Internet, right?

Yep. That's the short answer. But, don't think that the Internet is the savior in raising revenue.

I'll excuse Internet-only companies from this segment. If you're Amazon.com or eBay.com, go ahead and skip to the test at the end of this chapter. This part is for the millions of brick-and-mortar companies that are not Internet-only.

If "New as a Way of Life" has to include the Internet, here's what the Internet can't do:

1. **Swamp you with new revenue**. Grabbing big revenue chunks from the Internet doesn't just happen by accident. You just don't put up a website and get deluged with new revenue.

2. **Setting up and maintaining a website is cheap**. It can be cheap, really cheap. If your website is mainly informational, you could set it up for less than $100. If it's more complicated, and has thousands of items for sale, it could cost you millions.

I'll give you examples of two minor-league baseball teams in the Texas league. We would consider these teams small businesses. Both teams wanted to have a presence on the Internet.

One team spent $400,000 in developing its site and maintained it with three full-time employees. The purpose of the site was image, branding, and information. They also wanted to sell tickets on the site.

The other team, the Frisco RoughRiders, was the team I was associated with when I was president of Mandalay Baseball Properties. With this team, we spent $3,000 to create the site and had no full-time employees maintaining it. We did have different employees regularly contribute copy to the site, but the maintenance was outsourced to a company for $3,000 per year. Our sole purpose for the site was one thing: *Sell tickets*.

Whose site was prettier? The other guys', but not by a long shot.

Whose site brought in more revenue? The other guys brought in about $100,000 in ticket revenue. The Frisco RoughRiders brought in $700,000 in ticket revenue.

Why the huge difference? I think it goes back to the *purpose* of the site. The other team's purpose was more branding; ours was ticket sales. With our informational pages about the team and the players, we tried to funnel the reader to ticket sales.

When you came to the RoughRiders site you didn't have to search for ticket information. That information stared right back at you as soon as you came to our site. Additionally, we made a huge effort to drive people to our site. (See the next point.)

3. Getting people to your website is easy. (Remember, these points are what the Internet *can't* do for you.) You can spend millions in developing a website, but those millions are wasted if you can't *drive* people to your site. Yes, you can get some folks via Google adwords, but I'm talking about something even more aggressive (and less expensive).

With our minor-league baseball team, the Frisco RoughRiders, we wanted to drive website traffic, but we didn't want to spend much money. I think it's easier for a baseball team to do that than most other small businesses. After all, our customers are *fans*.

Here's how we drove traffic:

- **Our direct response ads in the newspaper.** We spent this advertising money whether there was a website or not. You can see the types of ads we ran in chapter 11. In the past, we encouraged people to phone in an order; now we were encouraging folks to go online and order. However, when they did go online, we didn't make it difficult for them to find the offer. Believe me, you couldn't miss how to order tickets.

- **Game program.** We handed out a free game program to every man, woman, and child that attended the game. It was filled with up-to-the-game info about the team and its players. We inserted our website address on every page. In the short bios about the players, we inserted our website address so that the reader could find

out more about that player. Our game program was thirty-two pages; our website was listed in many different ways about 100 times.

- **I would have put the website on our uniforms.** That wasn't allowed, of course, but we put our website on everything else.

Our Internet efforts, however, became stifled a bit when the sites of all minor-league baseball teams were corralled by Major League Baseball. The sites became more informational sites with a ticket component. We no longer controlled our site, and many of the things that we had done went by the wayside.

The lesson I learned about websites is a simple one: What is the purpose of the site? Simple question, eh? Well, if the purpose happens to be *revenue,* what part of your site isn't working toward that purpose? (By the way, my personal website is jonspoelstra.com. What do you think its purpose is?)

Another Writing Assignment

Get out that piece of paper you have in your shirt pocket — you know, the piece of paper that says, "What's it gonna take . . . ?" In the margin, write: "New as a Way of Life." You don't have to write the rest; you'll know what it means. Just put it back in your pocket and keep it with you.

Next time you pull that piece of paper out of your pocket, look at your own handwriting: "New as a Way of Life." Ask yourself: Is new becoming my way of life? Or am I doing the same-old same-old? After a few weeks of this, I believe New as a Way of Life will start to become part of *your* life.

A SIMPLE TEST YOU CAN TAKE

1. What's new?
   a. Not much.
   b. Nuthin'.
   c. Got a day and a half? I'll tell you about it.

2. Inventing new ways to market your product —
   a. takes too much time. (True/False)
   b. is unnecessary; your marketing efforts are just fine right now. (True/False)
   c. is impossible; there's nothing new under the sun about marketing your products. (True/False)

3. List up to three new marketing projects you'd like to start during the next nine months.

   a. _____

   b. _____

   c. _____

4. On that piece of paper in my shirt pocket, I have written "New as a Way of Life." (True/False)

Answers

1. I hope you answered "c." You'd be much more interesting. In fact, if we run into each other at some airport, I might not have a day and a half to listen to your new stuff, but you can start to tell me. Who knows, my flight may be delayed, or we might find ourselves sitting next to each other on a flight to Tokyo. We "gain" a day flying over there, you know.

2. The answer to all these questions is, of course, false. If you're not afraid of the new, then you will learn that inventing new ways to market your product —

    a. doesn't take too much time,

    b. can work even better than the old ones, and

    c. is entirely possible; there are always new ways you haven't thought of yet.

3. If you filled out just one line on this question, then congratulations! You've taken your first step in New as a Way of Life. Your revenue will increase, you'll have more fun, the staff will become more enthusiastic, and the boss will love you more and give you a ton of stock options.

4. C'mon, don't stop writing now. Go ahead, write down "New as a Way of Life" on that piece of paper in your shirt pocket. That little phrase can serve as a gentle reminder in the morning, during the day, in the evening. New as a Way of Life.

Time After Overtime

As you can probably tell, I'm a big fan of New as a Way of Life. I even wrote a book about it — *Success Is Just One Wish Away.* This is not a marketing book; it's a business fable. *The One-Minute Manager* was a business fable on how to manage people; *Success Is Just One Wish Away* is a business fable on how to stir the passion in your job. The book has sold decently, with especially big results in bulk sales after a company executive reads the book and recommends it to his colleagues as the perfect book to get people thinking New as a Way of Life. You can buy the book at Amazon.com. Or you can read the first chapter for free on Findsuccess.net.

CHAPTER 9

The Idea Champion

In the mid 1990s, while walking down a Tokyo street, I saw a huge digital clock. It told the time, of course, but it also displayed another number. Beside this number were some Japanese characters I couldn't read, but the number was plainly 1703.

The next day I passed by the clock again. This time the number read 1702. I stopped and in my halting Japanese asked a passerby what the number stood for. "It's the number of days until the new millennium," he explained. "Ah so des," I replied. "I understand."

The idea of a backwards calendar intrigued me. In this country, of course, we're accustomed to counting down our shopping days to Christmas. I don't know what the significance of the countdown was for the Japanese company that owned the clock, but as president of the New Jersey Nets, it gave me an idea: why not a backwards marketing calendar?

Pro sports is a seasonal business. Most of its revenues are generated in the six-month off season, when season tickets and sponsorships are sold. This window can be lengthened by starting marketing earlier. At the Nets, we started marketing tickets for the next season during the final two months of our current season. This gave us an eight-month marketing window.

As a marketing specialist, I felt we were frittering away some key marketing days during the front end of that window. After all, with eight months to sell tickets and round up sponsors, nobody felt guilty if not much happened in the first few weeks. We had plenty of time to make up for it. But toward the end we always wished we had a few more days before the season began.

Our backwards calendar helped us solve this problem. We set up a backwards calendar in the marketing department. It was like an ordinary tear-sheet desk calendar, but without a date — just a number for each weekday (weekends and

holidays didn't count), starting March 1 and ending November 2, the date of the regular season opening game. As we tore off each workday's sheet, the countdown number decreased by one. This reminded us from day to day that there was a time limit on our marketing. June 15? Nope, just the number 96, as in days to go. August 12? Just 56 marketing days left till tipoff.

Our ticket salespeople, who worked on commission, earned 80 percent of their income during this hectic marketing season. Thus, a day off in our marketing season was a day without pay. Suppose you wanted to take off the last half of August and go to the Jersey Shore to drink beer and ogle. Subtract 10 marketing days. Instead of 50 days, you had 40 left to sell tickets and make money. That meant a 20 percent pay cut for the rest of the marketing season. Was it worth it? The backwards calendar made you think.

We found our backwards marketing calendar useful in other areas. When we revised our group ticket marketing, we outlined all the steps we had to take. The most important step, and the one that would take longest, was to build a database of mailing addresses. We estimated that this task would take two months. Two months did not mean 60 days; it meant only 42 marketing days. So we started our backwards marketing calendar for this task at 42. At the same time, we were designing our catalog and deciding on the ticket packages to offer. By the time we were tearing pages 3, 2, and 1 off our 42-day backwards calendar, we were ready to go to press. A few days after that, the catalog was in the mail.

I never learned why that electronic calendar in Tokyo was counting down the days to the year 2000. But it did give us an idea that helped us avoid being fooled by time — the backwards marketing calendar.

You can be sure that one place I'll visit on my next trip to Tokyo will be that office complex. Will the countdown number then be to the next millennium? That would be — let's see — somewhere around 328,500 days. Now let me figure the number of marketing days. . . .

Crazy Ideas Welcome Here

At one of the Think Tanks that I used to run, we came up with an outrageously great idea — an idea that would knock your socks off. But we didn't run with that idea.

The reason?

We all got caught up in the day-to-day challenges of doing our jobs. There was no time to flesh out this great idea.

The next year when we held the Think Tank, that outrageously great idea resurfaced. This time, however, we came up with an even better idea. This better idea was the Idea Champion.

Let me explain.

During my second year at the Portland Trail Blazers, we held our first annual marketing Think Tank. Our mission: Come up with ideas that would improve what we did for a living. We drove to the Oregon coast and locked ourselves up in a scenic lodge for two days just to talk ideas.

In the two weeks before the Think Tank started, each participant (there were only five of us then) was required to write down five ideas a day. The only restriction on the ideas: no restriction. An idea could be anything that seemed to apply, even remotely, to our marketing. If each person did this, and didn't think on the weekends, he would come armed with fifty ideas. These fifty ideas were his *private idea bank*. I didn't collect the ideas and photocopy them; each person would reach into his idea bank when he saw it was appropriate.

If an idea's a *crazy* idea, don't stand up and cheer just yet. The crazy idea had to be nurtured and discussed. The discussion wouldn't be on why we couldn't use the idea, but how we could shape it so that it would work.

I was always surprised at how each idea always led to another and another. The first year, I took sparse notes. I just wallowed in the flow of ideas. It was wonderful. But that was a mistake on my part; there were a lot of great ideas, but not much follow-through.

We continued our Think Tanks even as the Blazers' marketing department grew to over twenty people. With more people, however, the Think Tanks became a little unwieldy, so we broke up into four teams of five people each. Three other marketing staff members and I were team moderators.

Our Think Tanks became more structured. Unlike the first few Think Tanks, we began to develop particular topics. One of these was this question: "How do we expand our radio network?"

You'd be amazed at how many terrifically outrageous suggestions that question produced. The most outrageous? "Why don't we buy our own satellite to transmit the games to the network?"

At the time, this was a truly crazy idea. No other team used satellites. Teams that had radio networks used telephone lines to transmit their broadcasts.

The satellite idea, as everyone now knows, was a great idea — maybe a little ahead of its time, but one that had real potential for expanding our radio network. We could broadcast our games to Idaho or Hawaii, Alaska or Nebraska, and not have to pay expensive long-distance telephone charges.

This was the idea that we sat on for a year. The following year, telephone rates went up. The satellite idea resurfaced. This time, we assigned an Idea Champion to it.

The Idea Champion as Czar

The Idea Champion served as shepherd, sponsor, chief operating officer, even semi-czar, for an idea. It was the Idea Champion's responsibility — as well as duty and honor — to do whatever it took to bring that idea to life. The Idea Champion didn't have to be the one who came up with the original idea — just someone who would passionately breathe life into it.

Each idea came with a small discretionary budget. If the Idea Champion needed help, he or she could recruit anybody from the company. As the idea started to take form,

the Idea Champion would keep me up to date on the progress. The Idea Champion and I were, in effect, co-CEOs of
the idea.

Being an Idea Champion doesn't mean dropping all
responsibilities. It's more like taking on a hobby — something you do in your spare time, before or after hours, on the
weekend, sandwiched into other daily tasks. Does this sound
like a burden? You'll be surprised at how readily you can find
the time for it without sloughing your regular duties.

I met frequently with each Idea Champion to monitor
progress, tweak the idea and keep it on track, and decide
whether it should get extra money or be mothballed. An idea
that was shelved wasn't automatically considered a failure.
It might just be dormant, and perhaps later could be drawn
out of its cocoon to become a butterfly.

Our Idea Champion for the satellite network was Berlyn
Hodges. Now, you'd think that with a satellite network we'd
pick somebody who was a real techie. Berlyn's principal
experience before he joined our marketing department was

being the trainer of a hockey team — not
exactly a Bill Gates or Paul Allen type of
techie. But Berlyn was a great organizer
who could transform batches of obscure
facts into a big picture that was clear
and bright and comprehensible.

Within six months, Berlyn had the
satellite radio network up and running.
We had installed satellite dishes at each
of our twenty-two existing network
radio stations and nine new stations.
The initial cost was $250,000, but we saved $70,000 per year
in telephone line charges. We also rented our dishes to other
fledgling networks for $100,000 per year. So, instead of our
games sounding as though they were being broadcast during
a hurricane, our satellite transmissions were crystal clear.
We had eliminated our telephone transmission costs and,

after a couple of years, were showing an annual profit of $100,000 from renting our satellite time.

The concept of the Idea Champion arose as a way to implement our primary idea — satellite-link broadcasting — but it was an even more far-reaching and useful invention. In the years and organizations that followed, any idea we felt worth pursuing was assigned an Idea Champion.

New Ideas as a Way of Life

The Think Tank and Idea Champion worked so well for the Blazers that I took those ideas with me when I went to the New Jersey Nets. I was curious to see how they would work in a different environment.

When I first walked through the Nets' doors, I felt like Dorothy in *The Wizard of Oz:* "Well, Toto, we sure aren't in Oregon anymore." The gloom was painted on the walls. The

Nets were failures, both on the court and in the front office. The staff seemed covered with scar tissue. They had been ordered not to try anything new, and they followed those orders faithfully. One of the owners told me, "These people are lazy and stupid. Fire anyone you want. Fire all of them."

Nobody got fired. The staff, many of whom I found bright and energetic, responded big-time to Think Tanks and Idea Champions. We came up with some crazy, outrageous, terrific ideas. Within a year, New as a Way of Life had taken root, demonstrating the great advantages of the ideas I had imported:

1. **Active participation in New as a Way of Life.** You could try to mandate New as a Way of Life, but don't expect people to stand up and cheer. In a Think Tank, however, they are not just part of the process, they *are* the process — the thinking, the planning, the execution. They elect one of their own to be the Idea Champion — and choose New as a Way of Life as their own goal.

2. **A natural source of good ideas.** Bouncing ideas off others is more creative than sitting alone in your office thinking. It's the difference between the applause of twenty people and the sound of one hand clapping. Good ideas get refined, and "crazy" ideas can be turned into workable ideas in a Think Tank. Workable ideas become successful ideas under the guidance of an Idea Champion.

3. **A training ground for weekly good ideas.** The annual Think Tank was great for spurring creativity, but I thought, Why wait a year? Problems cropped up all the time. Instead of keeping myself up at night worrying about solutions, why not Think Tank it? I met with marketing staff twice a week to solve problems as they arose. When a solution was found, an appropriate Idea Champion usually came with it.

Turning Awful into Awesome

You've heard people say that there's "no such thing as a bad idea." Don't believe it. There are some truly awful ideas. At our Portland Trail Blazer Think Tanks there was one guy, Mick Dowers, who was the best I have ever seen in consistently coming up with terrible ideas. It was uncanny how consistently he came up with horrendous ideas. He was a treasure-trove of awful ideas. And he wasn't kidding; he was as sincere as a person visiting the pope. At first, folks would laugh, or groan, or just shout out, "No mas."

There was genius, however, in Mick's awful ideas. After awhile, we found that *if we reversed his idea*, completely twisted it around (sometimes forcibly), it turned out to be a pretty good idea.

If we reversed it, stretched it, and then stomped on it, it was *a great idea*, a breakthrough idea. This got me to thinking:

> If the idea doesn't cause you to fall down laughing or groan-like-you-got-kidney-stones, then the idea probably isn't of the breakthrough variety.

Cherish the awful idea, but be concerned with who presents it. A domineering person who is emotionally attached to a bad idea can often browbeat others into agreement. This is when, as a Think Tank moderator, you need the wisdom of King Solomon. You can't say, "What a stupid idea!" Instead, you must take that stupid idea and divert that person's energy and passion to an idea that will work.

This isn't easy. I often manage it by saying, "That's an out-of-the-box idea. How can we modify it, change it, add to it?" Then I suggest something different, perhaps even the opposite of the idea. But that's how good ideas are discovered: by association, even with opposites.

Who to Cheer For

Cheer for the participants in your Think Tanks. Stand up and cheer for the Idea Champions. They will become the engine that drives New as a Way of Life, and they will bring you more revenue than you could ever have imagined.

And cheer for yourself. It's fun and rewarding to be present when new ideas are being born.

A SIMPLE TEST YOU CAN TAKE

1. Who is worthy of being an Idea Champion?
   a. You.
   b. The dumbest person on your staff.
   c. The star of your staff.
   d. The laziest person on your staff.
   e. The janitor in your building.
   f. All of the above.
   g. None of the above.

2. What's a bad idea good for?
   a. A few laughs.
   b. A few groans.
   c. A great idea.
   d. All of the above.
   e. None of the above.

Answers

1. f. All of the above. You might think this is a trick question. Would I do that to you? Of course not. So how do I explain letting the laziest or the dumbest on your staff become an Idea Champion? Or even the janitor, for crying out loud?

The most important part of being an Idea Champion isn't brains or work ethic — it's passion. If the least intelligent person on your staff volunteers to champion an idea and shows some passion about it, let that believer run with it. It might call for a little more guidance from you, but it will be worth your time. Along the way you may be pleased to discover that your "dumb" staffer *is* dumb — like a fox.

The laziest person on your staff can be a fine Idea Champion. Laziness usually indicates lack of interest. When a lazy person volunteers to be an Idea Champion and shows some passion, be delighted; it might be just the spark needed to give that person energy and enthusiasm.

The janitor? If the janitor volunteers to be an Idea Champion, consider yourself blessed.

With each of these folks, you'll spend a little more time assisting and monitoring. That's okay. They will become living advocates of New as a Way of Life.

2. d. All of the above. Sometimes, when you hear a really stupid idea, it's hard not to laugh until you hurt — or groan until you feel intense pain — but that's part of the creative process. As you know, I have a rule about great ideas: If people don't fall down laughing, it's probably not a breakthrough idea. So laugh, groan, and know that you're on the path to a great idea.

CHAPTER 10

Levels of Cream

R ed Hots! Red Hots!!"
"Who wants a beer?"
"Get your scorecard here!"
That's what you used to hear when you went to a baseball game. But things change, and after the '60s, the Red Hots (hot dogs) began to morph into a whole menu of fast food: nachos, sushi, pizza, beef balls. Beer cups became buckets. The scorecard that used to fit in your pocket grew into a five-dollar "program" as thick as a small-town phone book and stuffed with ads, inside which you could sometimes find the player lineup.

When I became president of the New Jersey Nets, we decided to turn the clock back a bit — not on the food or the beer, but on the game program. We took it back forty years, then added a neat twist to it: we gave it away free.

It came to me the night my wife and I attended a Broadway play in New York City. When we entered the theater, they handed us a small publication, about the size of a *TV Guide*, called *PlayBill*. Inside was a digest of the acts and actors. In the ten minutes before the curtain rose, I was able to read as much about the play as I wanted to know.

Driving back to New Jersey after the show, I thought, Why can't we do a *PlayBill* for our basketball games? One obvious reason was that no one was doing it. Every team in the NBA had an agreement with *Hoop* magazine to produce thick, magazine-like game programs. However, our agreement had expired. If we wanted to, we could replace *Hoop* and do our own version of *PlayBill*. We'd call it *PlayBall*.

PlayBall would be perfect for our fans. Instead of paying $4–$5 for a magazine, our fans would get *PlayBall* for free. Inside would be the information that the fans wanted: names and numbers of the players, some *USA Today*–style information about the game, and the most recent statistics. All for free.

The next day, I did the numbers. We were getting $70,000 a year from *Hoop*. Selling ads in our own *PlayBall,* we could make ten times as much — $700,000. The fans would benefit, and we'd make out like bandits.

I told *Hoop* magazine what we were going to do.

They said we couldn't do it.

I asked why.

"All the teams in the NBA work with us," they said, "and you'd be the only team that doesn't. That's not very smart, is it?" When they said that, I knew for sure our *PlayBall* idea was a great one.

They offered to increase our rights fee to $100,000.

I told them no.

"$150,000," they said. "That's more than any team in the NBA makes with us."

I told them I wasn't trying to negotiate a better deal. This sort of stumped them. Regardless of their offer, we were going to do *PlayBall,* because it was better for the fans. Only one out of thirty-five fans attending a game bought *Hoop*; every fan would get *PlayBall* free.

This stumped them again.

I did, however, offer them a compromise. We would continue to distribute *Hoop* magazine for them at the games, but I wanted to change the name to *Hoop Annual,* turn it into a team yearbook, and sell it to fans, like a fancy souvenir program for a Broadway play. They agreed, but they did a shoddy job of it. They lacked a burning desire to be in the "annual" business.

PlayBall was a rousing success. The fans loved it. We quickly sold all the advertising.

Other teams saw our *PlayBall.* They examined our ad rate card and did the math. Within a year, five more teams were doing their own versions of *PlayBall.* It spread to the National Football League, then to the National Hockey League.

As the trend picked up steam, I thought of *Hoop* magazine. It was time for them to start thinking about Marketing Outrageously.

The Marketing Churn

"The cream always rises to the top." You've heard that saying, haven't you?

The second person to have said that, I think, was a marketing person, talking about customers. (The first was a milkmaid.)

The marketing person added, "In fact, there are *levels* of cream that have risen to the top."

Let's take an easy example of Levels of Cream. You can buy a Mercedes for $35,000 or $200,000. Either one will get you from Point A to Point B quickly, smoothly, and in style. Both do the job, but one costs six times as much as the other — the one that's faster, smoother, and more stylish. The $200,000 Mercedes buyer is the top Level of Cream.

In the sports business, we've grown up with Levels of Cream. At Madison Square Garden, you can buy a New York Knicks ticket for one game for $10. Or you can buy a ticket for $2,000. Both seats let you watch all the action, cheer when you want, and see who wins the game. The $10 seat is up in East Nosebleed; two grand gets you first row, right there in the players' armpits.

Many companies allow Levels of Cream to happen naturally, like — well — cream rising to the top. The Levels of Cream principle is so easy to understand that you might be inclined to take it for granted. Don't let that happen. My preference is to develop a specific marketing strategy to increase your Levels of Cream.

The first time I consciously skimmed the top Levels of Cream was with the Portland Trail Blazers.

It was the early 1980s. All-sports cable channels were extending their tendrils into homes throughout the country. New York City had two — MSG and Sports Channel. Regional all-sports channels across the country were paying pro teams amazing fees for the right to cablecast their games.

However, in little Portland, Oregon — the twenty-third largest market, with only one major pro sports team — there wasn't much interest from regional sports packagers. We would have to carve our own path through the cable wilderness. (After all, we were the Trail Blazers.)

Our cable consultant recommended that we create our own all-sports channel and air at least 180 events. We would acquire the cablecast rights for Oregon State University and University of Oregon basketball games, Portland Winter Hawks (minor league) hockey, and Portland Beavers (minor league) baseball, import some major-league baseball games, and, of course, some Portland Trail Blazers games. His reasoning was that consumers were willing to pay $12 a month for specialty channels like HBO and all-sports channels, but you had to provide a lot of programming.

I did the numbers. The cost of producing 180 events was astounding. We'd have to commit hundreds of thousands of dollars. Then we'd have to split subscriber revenue 50-50 with the cable company. In other words, we'd pay almost all the costs and get only half of the revenue. We would also have to allow for "churn" — that is, turnover: pay channels typically lose 10 percent of their subscribers per month. This kind of math didn't appeal to us.

"What the fans really want," I said to Blazers owner Larry Weinberg, "are Portland Trail Blazer games. All the other stuff is just to give the appearance of value for the monthly outlay of $12."

"What do you suggest?" Larry asked.

"That we skim the Levels of Cream," I said.

"Explain."

We were selling out every home game we played. (In fact, in my eleven years with the Blazers, we sold out every home game.) When cable was new, some thought if you cablecast a home game you'd cannibalize your ticket-buying customers. We were willing to risk money, but not our gate receipts.

Some teams sold the cablecast rights to all of their games, both home and away, but we were already making a fortune telecasting our best twenty road games in-house. All that was left for cable was our twenty-one worst road games and all forty-one home games.

"Let's do what we do best," I said. "Let's take our top twelve home games — games like the L.A. Lakers with Magic Johnson and the Boston Celtics with Larry Bird — games that have the biggest demand. Let's put those into a package and sell it the way we sell our ticket packages."

"What's the price?"

"Our consultant says cable consumers will pay only $12 a month for pay channels. We have to get away from that model and think in terms of ticket packages. A reasonable price for ticket packages could be $120. Cash or credit card. And just like season tickets, you can't cancel once you get them."

"No churn," Larry said, smiling.

The $120 price point by itself wasn't exorbitant. However, if you compared $10 per game with what other teams were doing with their cable partners, it was outrageous. Those teams were getting about $1 a game per household. We'd get $10, but from fewer households. We were scooping up the top Level of Cream, the fans who were willing to pay a lot more. By targeting fewer households, we were confident we wouldn't cannibalize our ticket sales at the arena.

Pay-per-view was also becoming available, so if you didn't want to buy our cable package, you could buy the games one at a time at a truly outrageous price — $17 per game. A still higher Level of Cream.

We cut deals with all the Portland-area cable companies. The Blazers would do all the marketing, the cable companies would air the games. Instead of the usual 50-50, we negotiated an 80-20 split of revenues — 80 percent to us, because we were doing the marketing. We would also control our cablecast ad slots.

As part of our deal with the cable companies, we sent a mailing to all cable subscribers. This pulled about the same percentage as any direct mail piece, but that was okay: it enabled us to ferret out the true-blue Blazer fans who had cable.

Levels of Cream, however, works best when you know who the customer is. We compiled a list of people who had somehow indicated an interest in the Trail Blazers — people who signed up for a sweepstakes with a Blazer sponsor, fans who called our office to get a pocket schedule. When we mailed these folks our cable offer, we found our top Levels of Cream.

One of the highest response rates was from our current season ticket holders. Many of these fans shared their tickets with clients. They hated to pass up the big games, but a key client was a key client, and sometimes the client needed to see a Lakers or Celtics game. Now season ticket buyers wouldn't have to miss those games — they could order our cable package and watch them at home. The next year, we offered combo packages: you could go to some games at the arena and watch others on cable.

Because we featured our biggest and most important games in our cable package — the games that you really wanted to see in person — we saw no drop-off whatsoever in attendance at the arena. In fact, it could be said that with our pay-per-view cable "ticket," we expanded our attendance from the sold-out arena of 12,888 to over 30,000.

Let Them Spend More

Minor-league baseball teams don't have much variance in the price of their tickets. At many games you can pay as little

as $7 for a ticket, or spring for the highest price of $11. The ballparks are a lot smaller than major-league ballparks, of course. Instead of having 45,000 seats like MLB stadiums, there are usually about 7,000. One way of looking at that is there are 38,000 *worse* seats in an MLB ballpark; every seat in a minor-league ballpark is close to the action. So, how in the world could we capitalize on Levels of Cream for a minor-league baseball team.

Our experiment in Levels of Cream for a minor-league baseball team started in Dallas, Texas. Mandalay Baseball Properties bought a team in the Texas league and moved it to Frisco, Texas, a northern suburb of Dallas. Dallas is, of course, an upscale market and the home of the Dallas Cowboys, the Texas Rangers, the Dallas Mavericks, and the Dallas Stars. Truly a major-league market. Additionally, high school and college football is huge in Dallas.

The city of Frisco built a new stadium to house our Double-A minor-league baseball team. Could Levels of Cream work here, or were we just dreaming? Oh, by the way, the economy was awful in Dallas at that time. The Internet bubble had popped; IPOs were laying dead on the ground all over the place. Office parks in Richardson were as empty as ghost towns.

Well, here's how we priced our tickets. You could get a ticket for as low as $5. That was similar to most other minor-league teams. But, our highest price ticket was a lot different. $50. That's $50 per ticket per game. There were 70 home games, so one season ticket would cost you $3,500.

The next highest priced ticket was $35. Then $18. Then $9. And last, $5.

Why in the world would somebody pay $50 for a ticket to a minor-league baseball game? Well, the $50 ticket certainly wasn't right for everybody. But we weren't looking for everybody at this price point. We were looking for the top Level of Cream.

Here's why it was right for certain folks:

1. **Business entertainment in your neighborhood.** The concept of business entertainment is basically this: out-of-the-office bonding with a current customer or prospective customer. It can be lunch or golf or a baseball game, but it needs to be out of the office. If you had a business in the

Frisco/Plano area and many of your accounts were nearby, it would make good sense to take your clients to a Frisco RoughRiders base-ball game. You could go to a Texas Rangers major-league baseball game, but getting there from North Dallas is a nightmare. I've driven it. The drive to Minneapolis, Minnesota, seems easier. So, if it's business entertainment, why not stay in your own backyard?

2. **Predictable expenses.** We called these $50 tickets Founders memberships. You see, with each Founders Club membership, you would receive a free upscale all-you-can-eat buffet at every game. This included free wine, beer, soda,

water, coffee, tea. The buffet was located on the second deck behind home plate. It had beautiful sight lines to watch the game. It was air-conditioned, and in Texas during the summer, that counts. You also got free parking and free game programs. If you had one of these tickets, you could leave your wallet at home. In a lousy economy, having predictable expenses is vital.

Which priced ticket sold out first? Yep, you're right, the $50 ticket. And then the $35 ticket. In fact, we created a waitlist. The next year, we built two other restaurant areas just for our Founders Club members. One area featured Texas barbeque foods; the other area featured upscale ballpark food, like grilled cheeseburgers and hot dogs. Then we added a dessert bar. Free drinks

like wine, beer, soda, and water were available at these restaurants too.

If you had a Founders Club ticket, you could visit all of
our restaurants.

Bribing the Stomach

A naysayer out there could say that we weren't really selling
$50 tickets — we were just bribing somebody's stomach.
Well, sure, the food and drink did cost us about $15 per per-
son. So, I guess you could say that we were selling a $35 ticket
plus a $15 dinner. The average price for a ticket to a minor-
league baseball game is about $9, so for this Level of Cream,
we were getting almost four times that. That's working the
Levels of Cream to its best.

SEARCHING FOR LEVELS OF CREAM

Whenever I consult for a
company that badly needs
to boost revenue, I look to
Levels of Cream. It usually
doesn't take long to find
them. I seek answers to just
two questions:

1. Are the names of your
customers available? (In other
words, is the targeted segment
easily identifiable?)

2. If we put together a special package, would some of your customers be willing to spend a lot more?

If both of those questions can be answered with a YES!, then roll up your sleeves and get ready to do some Levels of Cream marketing.

A SIMPLE TEST YOU CAN TAKE

1. What are two important ingredients for Levels of Cream marketing?

a. _____

b. _____

2. The cream will naturally rise to the top and identify itself. (True/False)

Answers

1. a. *Are the names of your customers available?* The names are, of course, absolutely essential. Many companies making products to be sold by retailers don't know the names of their customers. This severely limits their ability to market Levels of Cream. Manufacturers who sell directly to customers know those names. This makes the next answer even more interesting.

b. *If we put together a special package, would a portion of the customers be willing to spend a lot more?* This requires creative thinking, which I've done with pro sports teams and other companies on countless occasions. For instance, in working with minor-league teams, I've said, "There is a company in this market that is willing to spend more on a sponsorship with your team than you could ever imagine." In a case like that, we would know the name of that potential big-spending sponsor because it would be a prominent company in the area. All we had to do was come up with the best sponsorship package that company had ever seen. In a medium-sized market, a minor-league baseball team's biggest local sponsor spent $25,000 a season. We designed a bigger and far better package that would cost $195,000. We sold seven of them.

2. False. This is a trick question. The cream in any business will indeed rise to the top, but it won't necessarily identify itself. A marketer has to be alert for marketing possibilities, then prepare and test some Levels of Cream marketing.

CHAPTER 11

Don't Throw Your Money into a Tornado

I've got a warped perspective on advertising: I think advertising should get results you can feel. Don't give me any of that image or identity stuff; I want revenue that I can track to the ad. Anything less is, to me, like throwing my money into a tornado and hoping for the best.

You might ask me: "How much revenue would make you happy?" Well, I've got a simple little formula for that: $4-to-$1. I call it The Ratio. For every dollar I spend on an ad, I want to see four dollars in revenue as a direct result.

We used The Ratio when I started consulting with the hapless, hopeless New Jersey Nets in the early '90s. Many pro sports teams spent a half million dollars or more on advertising; the Nets spent a puny $100,000. As small as their ad budget was, they wanted to blow the whole thing on a billboard campaign featuring their latest slogan. As their consultant, I said no way.

Now, don't get me wrong. I'm a big fan of billboard advertising. We used it when I was general manager of the Portland Trail Blazers to promote our radio broadcasts. Here we didn't use The Ratio. We used billboards to remind drivers where they could *listen* to our games. And it wasn't our ad budget — it was the radio station's money.

I recommended that the Nets use their puny ad budget on newspaper ads, to sell ticket packages. Nothing flashy; each ad would be one-sixth of a page, with a headline, a picture, lots of words, and a toll-free number.

When the ad agency showed us the first ad, most people at the Nets said, "Too many words."

I asked, "Why do people buy a newspaper? For the pictures, or for the words?"

What we wanted to do was ferret out readers who were interested in the Nets or the NBA. We wanted to persuade them to pick up the phone and order a ticket package. Our sole measurement for the ad's success was The Ratio. If it yielded better than $4-to-$1, it was a success; less, it was a failure.

The first ad pulled a $6-to-$1 ratio: for the $2,000 we invested in the ad, we got $12,000 in ticket sales. The next step was easy. We ran the ad again. We continued to run the ad twice a week in New Jersey's largest newspaper until the fans told us to stop. They told us to stop by *not* picking up the phone and ordering ticket packages at a $4-to-$1 ratio. Even then, we didn't stop advertising; we just inserted a new ad.

We ran ads in July, August, and September. Then, in October, we ran into a crisis. "We've run out of ad money," said Jim Lampariello, executive vice president of the Nets. "We've spent the hundred thousand we budgeted."

"What's the ratio?" I asked.

"A little better than $5-to-$1," Jimmy said.

"So, for about $100,000 in ads, we've received more than $500,000 in ticket orders."

Jimmy nodded.

"So why don't we just keep on running the ads?" I asked.

Jimmy explained to me that the chairman of the Nets, Alan Aufzien, was a tough money guy. Alan never exceeded a budgeted line item in any company he had ever owned. He was proud of that.

I went to see Alan. He saw me coming. As I walked into his office, he put up his hand like a traffic cop stopping a car. "We've spent our ad budget," he said. "I never go over a line item. Never."

"I know, Alan, but I want to talk to you about something else," I said. "I want to offer you a sporting proposition."

"What's that?" he asked.

"I want to run the ads and pay for them personally. You don't pay a nickel for advertising. I pay the whole thing."

Alan looked perplexed. "What's in it for you?" he finally asked.

"I'll pay for all the ads. I'll keep what comes in from the ad until I'm reimbursed. Everything above that, we'll split fifty-fifty."

Alan knew our ratio was better than $5-to-$1. "But you'll make a fortune on that deal," he said.

Let's check his math. For every $2,000 ad, we were getting about $10,000 in ticket sales. So if I bought the ad for the Nets, I'd keep the first $2,000 and we'd split the other $8,000. I'd make $4,000 every time I ran an ad.

"Yes, Alan, I'd make a fortune," I said. "But it should be the Nets making the fortune. As your consultant, here's what I recommend: Don't let me pay for the ads. Let the Nets go over budget and pay for the ads themselves."

Alan decided to break tradition. For the first time ever, the Nets went over budget. Way over. The Nets ended up spending more than $150,000 in advertising. The ratio stayed above $5-to-$1, a return of nearly $800,000.

But this was just the tip of the iceberg. By going over budget, the Nets entered a new world of ticket sales: database marketing. Now that ticket buyers had identified themselves by responding to our newspaper ads, we were able to upgrade over 25 percent of them to a bigger package during the same season. Another 25 percent upgraded to a bigger package the following season. Thus, the original $800,000 in revenue grew to more than $1,000,000 in ticket sales the following season. And this extra money didn't require us to spend a penny on advertising — just to write a letter. Since letters were far less expensive than ads, the ratio soared to almost $400-to-$1.

Just think, if Alan hadn't broken one of his own rules, he would have made a million-dollar mistake. Worse, he wouldn't even have known he'd made a mistake.

Big Bang on Ice?

Several years after the Edmonton Oilers sold Gretzky to the Los Angeles Kings, the Kings traded Gretzky to the St. Louis Blues for a bunch of unknown players.

The Oilers built a statue of Gretzky and hoped for the best. The Kings thought an image ad campaign would make up for the loss of Gretzky. It would have been better if the Kings had built a statue.

The Kings thought they could spend their way to a better image before the season started. They spent $1 million on TV ads in just the month of August to convince the people of Los Angeles that they should become hockey fans. They didn't feature star players in the commercials. They couldn't. They had traded the biggest star of all time. Instead, they used a theme: Real Hockey. The commercials were sort of artistic, like Nike ads, with the Kings' phone number flashed at the end in case you wanted to buy tickets.

Unfortunately, to most of the fans Real Hockey meant Wayne Gretzky, and Real Hockey had been traded to St. Louis. The result of the million-dollar ad campaign? Eight new season tickets sold — about $14,000. That's right, the Kings traded $1,000,000 for $14,000. For every dollar they spent on advertising, they got back about a penny and a half.

The Los Angeles Kings' mistake was that they didn't really understand advertising as another *marketing tool.* They thought advertising was — well, advertising, a way to influence the thought processes of consumers. They might have done that, but it certainly didn't lead to ticket sales. And if the advertising didn't lead to ticket sales, why spend the money? Some folks would say, "Image. Improve the image and sales will eventually come." Maybe. Maybe not.

Image advertising works best when a large percentage of the population uses a certain type of product — like soft drinks or cars or fast food or shoes. This wasn't the case with the L.A. Kings.

Because hockey is on the sports pages all winter long, you might think it's a popular consumer product. It isn't. In any major market in the country, fewer than 5 percent of the people attend a pro sports game, whether hockey, football, baseball, or basketball. The Los Angeles Kings tried to reach the masses of greater Los Angeles, but their target market was probably less than 2 percent of the population.

Well, you say, why not load up on mass advertising? Go after that 95 percent that aren't buying a ticket. Yeah!

Hold on to that checkbook. The Los Angeles Kings already had great awareness. After all, during their seven-month season, they were in the sports pages every day, TV news every night, and radio sports talk shows frequently; their games were on radio, TV, and cable; their fans wore Kings hats and jackets.

Instead of spending their entire $1 million ad budget in a single month, the Kings should have used half that amount for a year's worth of ads, the other half to hire more ticket salespeople to jump-start their business-to-business sales.

That's Right, I'm Biased

My thinking about advertising might, I admit, be a little flawed. You see, I've never worked with an advertising budget large enough to guarantee that sales would *eventually* come. Our advertising always had to show immediate results. Each advertising dollar had to be accounted for — you know, how many dollars did we get in return?

Yeah, I know that's simplistic, but that's why I put this disclaimer in here. If you've got a big ad budget, go ahead and spend it on image and identity. Yes, I believe it works. Look at Coca-Cola and Budweiser. But if you don't have a product with a large consumer acceptance, why ape the big guys? You might learn how to spend a little and get both image *and* immediate results.

Let's look at advertising as a marketing tool and see exactly how it can increase sales. To oversimplify again, there are two basic schools of advertising:

1. **Build Identity.** When Ford brings out a new Taurus, it spends a fortune telling consumers. TV commercials show the car whipping around corners on winding coast roads. Nice image. You never see new cars in their real-life habitat, panting like weary soldiers in rush-hour traffic.

Do the ads tell you much about the Taurus? Not really. It's new, it's cool, it's happenin'. Image, image, image. They don't even say where to buy one.

This identity-building process doesn't stop even when consumers are fully aware of the product. Think Coca-Cola. Coke's been the top-selling soft drink since forever. To stay there, Coke far outspends Pepsi in advertising, year after year.

How about Nike? That company took a mundane industry — gym shoes — and turned it into a lifestyle product. It's now socially acceptable to wear gym shoes almost anywhere outside the gym — a fashion revolution Nike ignited by spending a fortune on creative advertising.

2. **Buy Now.** Buy a Taurus *today;* buy a six-pack of Coke *today;* buy a pair of Nikes *today.* The cost of developing the identity for Taurus, Coke, and Nike was the responsibility of the manufacturer; the cost for getting consumers to buy today is the responsibility of the retailer.

How much identity is there in the car dealers' newspaper ads? None. It's all about price. When dealers get tired of hyping low price, they hype low price some more. When dealers make their own TV commercials, what do they emphasize? Price again. It's the same with retailers of Coke and Nike. One small picture of the product, the brand name, and price, price, price.

The purpose of featuring low price is, of course, to get the consumer to buy *now.* Don't wait — prices will go up — buy *now.*

Can one type of advertising work without the other? Sure. The Build Identity variety can work without the Buy Now ads. Coca-Cola proves it every day. If the Ford dealers didn't run local newspaper ads touting price, consumers influenced by Taurus TV commercials would somehow find their way to a Ford store.

However, the Buy Now variety couldn't work without the Build Identity. Picture a generic automobile, a nondescript box on wheels called "Car." Here's a local ad with a grainy picture of a boxy, gray Car. No scenic shots of Car amid redwoods or splashing through the surf. Ho-hum. Car sells for $3,000 less than Taurus. Will people abandon the Taurus and flock to the Car dealer? Not likely.

So it looks like I've talked myself into Build Identity. The only problem is that I've never had the ad budget to afford it. That's why I've always chosen to do both at the same time — Build Identity *and* Buy Now.

I could never afford to do Build Identity, but I could afford to do both. Let me give you an example. This example isn't from a famous team; it's from an obscure team, but the principles work wherever I've been.

Football with a Roof

A new pro sports team moved to Portland in 1997. This wasn't the Cleveland Browns moving to Baltimore with all that hoopla and controversy. These folks were the Memphis Pharaohs of the Arena Football League, and one day they just showed up in Portland calling themselves the Portland Forest Dragons.

Arena football ("football with a roof") is fun to watch. It may seem hard to believe, but there's more action, more bone-crushing tackles, in arena football than in the NFL. The field is fifty yards long instead of a hundred, teams field seven players instead of eleven, usually 100 points are scored per game.

Portland knew none of this.

Few in Portland had ever seen an Arena Football League game in person. Few Portlanders knew that the Pharaohs/Forest Dragons had a two-year losing streak going, an American record for most consecutive games lost in any pro sport, or that the Pharaohs had to move because of lack of community support. Few in Portland had even heard of the Pharaohs, much less any Pharaoh players, or any arena football players anywhere. There were no Joe Montanas, no Jerry Rices in arena football.

How could the Forest Dragons possibly succeed in Portland? A big wallet would certainly have to be part of the equation.

You'd think the owners would want to do at least two things:

1. **Spend big money on ads.** Because the Forest Dragons were bringing a new sport to a new market, they'd need a big ad budget just to educate potential fans that the team even existed and that arena football was indeed a sport. (It's strange how these things work, but if people don't know about a product, they don't buy it.)

2. **Start marketing early enough to make a difference.** When Peter Pocklington of the Edmonton Oilers hired my company to jump-start his season ticket sales, we had about nine months before the next season started — plenty of time to make a difference. However, to save money, the Forest Dragons decided to start late. Instead of nine months, or even six months, they thought it would be cheaper to do it in three months. Then they hired my company at the time, SRO Partners. They also created a very small ad budget, the equivalent of three full-page ads in Portland's daily newspaper, the *Oregonian.*

We quickly hired six young salespeople. Four would call on corporations, one would sell to groups, and one would take phone orders.

Then we started to spend the minuscule ad budget. The four salespeople calling on corporations would make sales with or without an ad campaign, but to sell Joe Fan, we would need to advertise. With our tiny ad budget, we decided we had to use both the Build Identity and Buy Now approaches:

1. **Build Identity.** In our ad, we explained the basics of arena football — you know, wide-open football, plenty of hits, lots of fun, close-up action.

2. **Buy Now.** Instead of discounting tickets, we used a premium — a genuine game ball — to catch the reader's attention and make him want to buy *right now.*

Know the first thing the Memphis owners said? "Too many words."

Sound familiar?

The owners felt that all we needed was an action picture and a phone number. I asked them the same question I asked

the New Jersey Nets owners: "Why do people buy newspapers? To look at the pictures?" If the ad were interesting enough, people would read the words. Without the words, we were missing the Build Identity part. If the owners had budgeted $500,000 for TV commercials showing the excitement, the hits, the cheering fans, then perhaps a picture-and-price newspaper ad would have worked for the Buy Now side.

We ran the small ad, three columns by eight inches. It cost $1,000. We sold $13,000 worth of tickets within three days, beating the heck out of our $4-to-$1 objective: The Ratio. We ran the ad again, same price, and grossed $8,000. The fifth time we ran the ad, the fans told us to stop — we received less than $4,000. So we started over with a new ad.

When we ran the first ad, the Forest Dragons had only a few no-name stragglers left over from Memphis. Soon, though, the team signed a few players Portlanders might recognize, so our second ad featured another Building Identity component — who to cheer for.

"Who to Cheer For" was certainly not a pretty ad — so ugly, in fact, that I considered not using it in this book. Too many words crammed into a small space with lousy pictures. But it got pretty results: better than $5-to-$1.

For the people who read the ads but didn't respond, we had at least started to Build Identity about the Portland Forest Dragons. They began to understand arena football, recognize that Portland had a team, and learn some of the players' names. We'd get them with the next ad. Or the one after that.

Spending less than $25,000, we were able not only to Build Identity for the Portland Forest Dragons but to generate $100,000 in Buy Now ticket sales directly attributable to the ads. And this didn't include revenue from our four-person sales force, which brought in about 80 percent of our season-ticket sales.

The Internet Can Goose Newspaper Ads

The newspaper business is a scary business nowadays. In the last decade, they've maintained a pace of losing 1 percent of their circulation per year. Each day fewer people go to their newspapers for news. Pretty bleak, eh?

Yeah, it's bleak if you're in the newspaper business. If you're an advertiser, however, I *still* find newspapers the most efficient ad medium for companies that don't have big ad budgets. Even with the shrinking circulation.

You just have to tweak a few things in your newspaper ads. Here are the tweaks:

1. **Change the goal of your ad.** The goal used to be to get the reader to react quickly to your offer. Either pick up the phone and order, or go to the store and buy. To do that, you would have to give the reader enough information to make the decision. Now, the goal is different. You don't have to give them enough information; you need to drive them to your website. You see, before buying a big ticket item (or even a medium or small ticket) folks will check out the product on the Internet. Have you purchased a car in the past few years? You probably first shopped on the Internet. So, now your ad has to be convincing enough to get the reader to go to your website. It still requires solid information, but it also leads the reader to a lot more information on the website.

2. **Don't lose them on your website.** How many times have you been led to a website and then couldn't find what you were looking for? That happens a lot. One way to handle that is to have a dedicated website for the ad.

Take a look at the ad below. It's for a minor-league base-ball team in Winston-Salem, North Carolina.

In the ad, please notice the website. That was not the team's regular website. It was a website created specifically for that ticket sales campaign.

We listed the website *four times* in the ad:

1. In the byline.

2. At the end of the body copy.

3. In the team information.

4. Last, in the caption. Captions are wellread, so this position might have driven more people to the website than the others.

The website had links to the team's regular website, but this website's sole purpose was to sell tickets. It was a simple website; on each page there was a prominent link to ordering a ticket package.

Essentially, our ad led interested folks to our brochure for buying tickets.

If you've got a big ad budget, go ahead, knock yourself out in spending it. If you've got a modest (or even teeny) ad budget, look to spend it in just two areas: (1) newspapers and (2) your website.

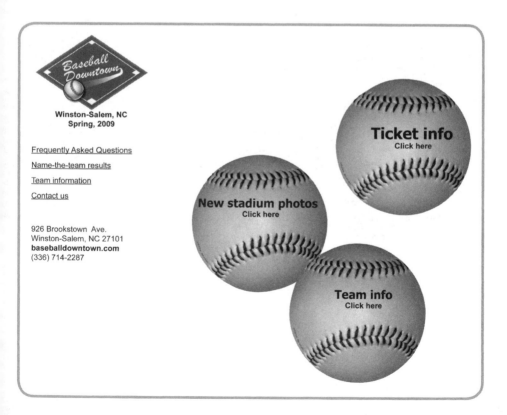

Winston-Salem, NC
Spring, 2009

Frequently Asked Questions

Name-the-team results

Team information

Contact us

926 Brookstown Ave.
Winston-Salem, NC 27101
baseballdowntown.com
(336) 714-2287

Your choices for tickets

You have more choices than you think.

Here's what you get to choose from:

• **Founders Club membership.** The Founders Club members get the best seat locations in the ballpark. You can choose seats in the first three rows between the dugouts. Or you can choose box seats on the second deck near the private Founders Club restaurant. These seats have four chairs surrounding a small table.

The Founders Club is a private restaurant in the stadium. It is in the second level, behind home plate, overlooking the diamond. Included in the Founders Club membership is an upscale buffet at each game, including wine, beer, soda and water. **Click here for more information.**

• **Choice seats.** You don't have to buy a full season ticket to get choice seat locations. We sell 'season tickets' in three ways: 1) Full season (70 home games), 2) Half season (35 home games) and 3) Partial season (18 home games) Prices range from just $9 to $11 each. **Click here for more information.**

• **Luxury suites.** You can purchase a suite for all home games or for a single game. **Click here for more information.**

The Founders Club

Winston-Salem, NC
Spring, 2009

Frequently Asked Questions

Name-the-team results

Team information

Contact us

926 Brookstown Ave.
Winston-Salem, NC 27101
baseballdowntown.com
(336) 714-2287

A Founders Club membership is where you have the best seats in the ballpark *plus* a private restaurant to go to before, during and after the game.

For the best seats in the house, we have a choice for you:

1. **Really close to the action.** These are reserved seats in the first three rows between the dugouts.

2. **Box seats on the second deck** near the private Founders Club restaurant. These seats have four chairs surrounding a small table.

Whichever seat location you choose, you still have access to the private Founders Club.

The Founders Club is located right behind home plate. It's on the second level and you get a terrific view of the game. You can watch the game and enjoy food and drinks in your air conditioned club. Specific seats are not reserved; this is like the restaurant in a club.

Each game night, you'll have an elaborate dinner buffet at no cost to you and your guests. This isn't typical ballpark/hot dog fare. We'll have different food themes throughout the season. **(Click here to see sample menus.)** Plus, you get complimentary beer, wine and soft drinks through the 7th inning.

Every time you take guests to our game, you won't have any additional costs. Everything is included in your membership: tickets, dinner, drinks, desserts, parking. **It's all-inclusive.** This is a great step to **cost certainty** while entertaining at a very high level.

When you leave the ballpark, you'll be the first to get to your car in your preferred parking spot.

The number of memberships in our Founders Club is highly limited. The cost for membership is $2,100 per seat per season. Partial membership starts at $510 per seat.

Type	Games	Cost per Membership	4 Memberships
Full	70	$2,100	$8,400
Half	35	$1,050	$4,200
Partial	18	$540	$2,160

This membership includes your Premier seat in our best seating section and full use of the Founders Club during the games.

You can reserve your Founders Club memberships by calling us or **clicking here.**

To order Founders Club
Click here

How to Count

Whenever we ran an ad, we'd see an immediate spike in the visits to the website and in orders. When we didn't run an ad, the website visits would plummet. We kept detailed reports on this data. At first, a majority of the orders that came in were by phone, but most of the people had told us that they had seen the new stadium renderings on the website. That told us that we needed to improve our Internet ordering system. Our Internet ordering wasn't as easy as ordering a book from Amazon. That was the ultimate goal, our "Amazon acid test."

Double-Duty Trade Ads

Some companies run ads in trade publications to Build Identity. Usually there's a picture, a headline, some bullet points, and a logo. The advertiser doesn't usually expect to sell anything with the ad, just raise awareness.

Remember, I believe advertising should produce results you can *feel*. On the limited budgets I usually find myself working with, every ad should pull double duty: raise awareness *and* ask for the order. We ran a trade ad in *Advertising Age* that did just that for the Portland Trail Blazers.

Advertising Age is a national trade publication of the ad industry, which in my mind includes the sponsorship industry. Tucked away in the Great Northwest, we were out of the mainstream national sponsorship prospects, whose ad agencies were clustered in New York, Chicago, and Los Angeles. We were making a fortune from our in-house radio and television broadcasts and our current sponsorships, but we were always looking for new sponsors.

Trade ads in *Advertising Age* are typically "awareness" ads — a picture, a headline, a few bullet points, and a logo. Yes, we wanted to create awareness of the Portland Trail Blazers, but we also wanted to Build Identity that we were a special sports team. A typical awareness ad *might* build some awareness, but it wouldn't tell our special story. Besides, we wanted to get some orders from our advertising.

Our ad layout was really pretty boring. It had no action picture of a basketball player. It didn't even have our logo. It had a lot of copy. So, the ad really looked gray. Here's what it said:

(Headline) Choose just one free booklet

(Subheadline) One could earn $300,000 in just a few days. The other could bring in over $13,000,000.

The ad then told about some of the successes of the Portland Trail Blazer sponsors. To get similar results, we offered free booklets: (1) Sports Sponsorship Case Studies or (2) Sports Sponsorship Evaluation. Pick just one.

Thousands of companies from around the country responded.

We tracked every written response, every phone call. The ad, which cost us $3,000, generated $880,000 in new sponsorships — $293 for every dollar we spent. We not only beat The Ratio, we boogied in its end zone.

Making the Wrong Assumptions

Marketers commonly make two wrong assumptions about advertising:

1. **You can't do Build Identity and Buy Now at the same time.** I usually hear this at the start of a consulting job. I prove it wrong every time I run an ad.

2. **People won't read a lot of copy.** This one's pretty silly. People read newspaper and magazine stories. They will read ad copy if (1) they have a modicum of interest in the product or service, (2) the ad catches their attention, and (3) the copy is interesting. If people aren't interested, then Build Identity won't create interest. I have no interest in dentures, so I skip right over denture ads.

If the ad doesn't catch a reader's attention or is boring, then I agree — people won't read the ad.

Making the Right Assumptions

Advertising is an important component of Marketing Outrageously. To make advertising really work for you, assume the following:

1. **You can spend less.** When you run an ad based on the revenue it brings you, rather than as just part of a mosaic, you'll find that you spend less money.

2. **You can Build Identity and Buy Now at the same time.** You may think you can come up with an exception to this, but I've never found one.

If you're with a mega-corporation that has a fortune to spend on advertising, you might not care about this "Build Identity and Buy Now while spending less" stuff. Go ahead and spend. Spend big. It's good for the economy — especially the media companies.

But if you're an entrepreneur without a huge ad budget, try it my way. You might find it outrageously enjoyable to spend less and have strangers call you up and beg to buy.

A SIMPLE TEST YOU CAN TAKE

1. What product wouldn't the Build Identity and Buy Now concept work for as either a consumer ad or a trade ad?

_____

2. You want to run a trade ad. You decide to try the Build Identity and Buy Now approach to get either an immediate order or a solid lead. Which of the following won't happen?

    a. Somebody in your office will say, "There are too many words in the ad. Nobody will read that."

    b. You'll get immediate orders or really solid leads.

    c. You'll track the results of each ad to answer one simple question: For each dollar you spent, how much money did you receive?

    d. None of the above.

Answers

1. You may have written, "Gum." What can you say about gum? Let's see — it tastes good; it's chewy. You know, I could almost agree with you. But what about Nicorette? Chew Nicorette and you'll quit smoking. Or chew sugar-free Dentyne and you'll lose weight, keep your teeth, smell good, and leap tall buildings in a single bound.

Well, then, how about — nose hair clippers? Forget it. Nose hair clipper ads have been in airline magazines for years. They Build Identity: For you older guys who are sprouting hair where you never expected to, these clippers do the job safely. Buy Now: Only $19.95! Call 1-800-NOSTRIL.

I say again: The Build Identity and Buy Now approach works for almost any product.

2. d. None of the above. The correct answer might also be "c." A lot of marketers don't want to track their ads. However, using the Build Identity and Buy Now approach, it is absolutely essential that you track the results.

You will, of course, run into resistance with this type of ad, but resistance from within is a major part of Marketing Outrageously. Come to expect it. Come to depend on it. When you don't get resistance, start wondering what you're doing wrong.

CHAPTER 12

The Rubber Chicken Method

Rick Benner was down for the count. After reviewing his season-ticket renewal figures in summer 1998, the president of the Sacramento Kings felt beat up — not physically, but emotionally. It looked like 4,000 of the Kings' season-ticket subscribers — 10 percent — would not renew.

Kings fans felt a little beat up, too. They had endured fourteen straight losing seasons, the longest any pro team had ever gone without coming out ahead. Until the summer of 1998, however, the fans had kept buying season tickets — better than 90 percent renewals every year, in fact.

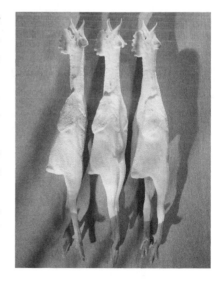

To make things even worse, the team could do nothing to improve itself. The NBA had imposed an indefinite labor lockout. NBA teams couldn't sign a free agent, couldn't trade. If you finished the season with a lousy team, you were stuck with a lousy team during the all-important marketing period. You had to market your lousy team without the one priceless tool that was available to pro sports teams: perennial hope that the team would get better.

The Kings had already sent three mailings to season-ticket holders who had not renewed. The fourth letter, according to the Kings' pattern, would be a "drop-dead" letter. This was a letter in wordy legalese, sent to a hundred or so nonrenewers to clear their seats for new buyers. It said, in effect, "You no longer have any rights to your season tickets. See ya."

As a marketing consultant to the Sacramento Kings, I was alarmed. This would be the last nail in the coffin for 4,000 season tickets. With 40 percent nonrenewals staring us in the face, how could we stop this death spiral? I felt that Kings fans were terrific fans, maybe the most loyal fans in the league. They had, after all, bought season tickets through fourteen straight losing seasons. But now 40 percent of them were saying, "Enough is enough!"

Those fans needed special attention — something to reassure them that management would somehow deliver a competitive team.

I went to Rick and asked him not to send the drop-dead letter. I suggested another approach. I showed him a letter I had drafted. Unlike the other letters, which had been written by accountants and lawyers and sounded that way, this letter was honest with the fan. It didn't hedge; it stated our problems — and solutions — in straightforward language.

Rick liked the letter. But, he said, there was one problem. "Our fans won't even open the letter. They never open any of our letters."

"That's because they were boring and vague," I said. "They were lousy reading. But I can get them to open this one. I'll guarantee it."

"How are you going to do that?" he asked. Then he remembered a story from my book *Ice to the Eskimos*. "Not the Rubber Chicken?"

I nodded. "The Rubber Chicken."

It was a rubber chicken, three feet long, that was stuffed into a tubular FedEx package. The chicken had on a little paper jersey. On one side, the jersey read, "Don't fowl out!"; on the other, "You're about to fowl out! However, you can avoid the bench and keep on playing. Just read the attached."

The "attached" was our letter, inside an envelope tied to the chicken's leg.

It took just one day to find out what the response would be. A few of our grumpier fans thought we had insulted them — but many of them renewed their season tickets anyway. They had read the letter and liked what we had to say. Many more fans were amused; they called us, laughing, to renew.

Some fans who had already renewed called and said, "How come I didn't get a rubber chicken?" We sent them their own personal rubber chicken.

A sports columnist at the local newspaper, the *Sacramento Bee*, got a rubber chicken:

> I've seen a lot of things in my day, Mister. I have seen grown men and women cry over games. I've seen courage and I've seen cowardice. I have seen feats of majesty and precociousness and minutiae and enduring value, all in the name of sports. In a reflective moment, I fancy that I've nearly seen it all.
>
> Then again, no NBA team ever sent me a rubber chicken in the mail.

The Rubber Chicken accomplished its mission. I'm pretty sure everybody who got a rubber chicken read the letter. They'd have to. If you received a letter attached to a rubber chicken, you'd probably read it too.

Did it work? It definitely helped. It cost us about $12 to send each chicken. We got 1,000 extra renewals, worth about $2.5 million in revenue.

And that — heh, heh — ain't chicken feed.

Rubber Chicken
Ad Theory

What do you think about my Rubber Chicken? A cheap marketing trick? Or a pretty neat idea, under the circumstances?

To me, the Rubber Chicken was neither. The Rubber Chicken was a subheadline.

A *subheadline?*

Yes, a subheadline. And the FedEx box was the headline.

A *headline?*

Let me explain. I think of a lot of marketing concepts in terms of an ad.

Now, before I go any further, here's a disclaimer. I'm going to talk about using words to help you market, but this chapter isn't a treatise on advertising. (If that's what you want, go to Amazon.com and type "advertising" in the search box. You'll get a list of 49,813 books.) It will, however, give you some useful guidelines for using words in Building Identity and Buy Now advertising and promotions.

Let's say you read a few of those books you found at Amazon.com. What would you learn? One book might say that the best headline needs to name one benefit of the product. Another book would say you have to have the product name in the headline. Advertising philosophies are all over the map. And they all work — if you've got lots of ad money in the budget.

But I've never had that luxury, so I see things a little differently. To me, the headline of an ad (the FedEx box) has only one purpose: to get the reader to read the subheadline. And the only purpose of the subheadline (the Rubber Chicken) is to get the reader to read the copy.

The product and the benefit are superfluous at this stage of the selling process.

Thus, the one purpose of the FedEx box was to get the recipient to open it and pull out the rubber chicken. And the one purpose of the rubber chicken was to make sure the letter got read.

A surprised Kings fan holding this scrawny rubber chicken would immediately notice two things:

1. The paper jersey that read, "Don't fowl out!"

2. The envelope attached to the leg.

Now, tell me, could you have *not* opened that letter? Nobody has that much willpower. So the subheadline (the Rubber Chicken) did its job. It got the reader to read the body copy — in this case, the letter.

The first paragraph in the letter also had a single purpose: to get the reader to read the second paragraph. Ditto the second, third, and succeeding paragraphs.

You don't have to worry about mentioning the product or company name or stating a benefit in any of these lead-in

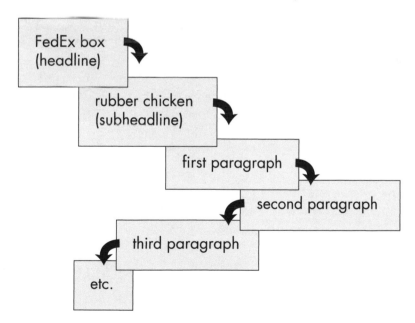

items. Just make sure each item creates enough interest to lead the prospect to the next item.

So when do we sell something?

The selling begins with the headline. For the Sacramento Kings, we created interest with the mysterious FedEx box. A soon-to-be-lapsed season-ticket holder would think, "What in the world could they be sending me?"

With the Rubber Chicken, we kicked interest to a whole new level, making it even more likely the reader would stick with it. Then, in the four-page letter, we gave the prospect several good reasons to renew.

To Build Identity, we itemized why the team was going to get better. We added credibility by guaranteeing this. Then we offered several reasons why the prospect should Buy Now.

Slippery Slide

The principles that led us to create the Rubber Chicken promotion also work with print ads. The headline should create enough interest to pull the reader to the subheadline, which should lead to the first paragraph, and so on. In a well-designed ad, the reader will pick up enough momentum to stay interested all the way to the end.

Remember, when you were a kid, how you used to climb to the top of that playground slide on a muggy summer day and rub sand on the hot metal to keep from sticking? Then you'd slide down, lickety-brindle, going faster and faster all the way to the bottom? In your ad, think of the headline and subheadline as sand on the slide. They make you read faster and faster, and before you know it, you've read the whole thing.

The year before the Sacramento Kings faced their huge desertion of season-ticket holders, they were trying to increase attendance. They ran the following ad, a typical one in pro sports, in the *Sacramento Bee*.

Do you see a slippery slide in this ad? Neither do I. Nor did the 400,000 readers of the *Sacramento Bee*. Did this ad Build Identity or make you want to Buy Now? Nope. It wouldn't even have made a good used-car ad: no price.

The Kings ran the ad twice. Here are the results:

AD RESPONSE						
Date	Medium	Ad title	Cost	Sales	Revenue	Ratio
8-25-97	*Sacramento Bee*	Season Tix	$1,527	1	$360	$0.24
8-28-97	*Sacramento Bee*	Season Tix	$1,527	1	$512	$0.34

You read the ratio right. For every dollar the Kings spent on the ad, they got twenty-nine cents in revenue.

We decided to try a different approach. In our first ad, we featured the greatest star attraction pro sports has ever seen — Michael Jordan. Why? Because the Kings were in turmoil.

- They had missed the playoffs the year before.

- Their star player at the time, Mitch Richmond, publicly said he wanted to be traded.

- Their free-agent power forward, Brian Grant, rejected the Kings' contract offer and signed with the Portland Trail Blazers.

- The Kings' owner got the city to guarantee a highly controversial $70 million loan to refinance the team and the arena.

So we featured Michael Jordan, Shaquille O'Neal, and a "new saint." The "old saint" was the former head coach,

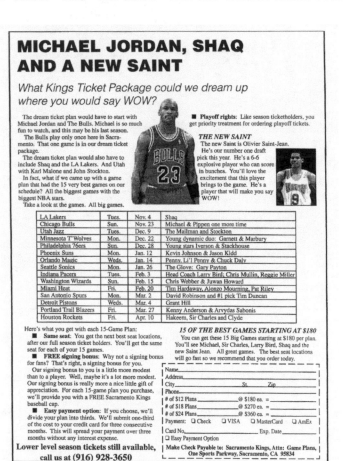

MICHAEL JORDAN, SHAQ AND A NEW SAINT

What Kings Ticket Package could we dream up where you would say WOW?

The dream ticket plan would have to start with Michael Jordan and The Bulls. Michael is so much fun to watch, and this may be his last season.

The Bulls play only once here in Sacramento. That one game is in our dream ticket package.

The dream ticket plan would also have to include Shaq and the LA Lakers. And Utah with Karl Malone and John Stockton.

In fact, what if we came up with a game plan that had the 15 very best games on our schedule? All the biggest games with the biggest NBA stars.

Take a look at the games. All big games.

■ **Playoff rights**: Like season ticketholders, you get priority treatment for ordering playoff tickets.

THE NEW SAINT
The new Saint is Olivier Saint-Jean. He's our number one draft pick this year. He's a 6-6 explosive player who can score in bunches. You'll love the excitement that this player brings to the game. He's a player that will make you say WOW!

LA Lakers	Tues.	Nov. 4	Shaq
Chicago Bulls	Sun.	Nov. 23	Michael & Pippen one more time
Utah Jazz	Tues.	Dec. 9	The Mailman and Stockton
Minnesota T'Wolves	Mon.	Dec. 22	Young dynamic duo: Garnett & Marbury
Philadelphia 76ers	Sun.	Dec. 28	Young stars Iverson & Stackhouse
Phoenix Suns	Mon.	Jan. 12	Kevin Johnson & Jason Kidd
Orlando Magic	Weds.	Jan. 14	Penny, Li'l Penny & Chuck Daly
Seattle Sonics	Mon.	Jan. 26	The Glove: Gary Payton
Indiana Pacers	Tues.	Feb. 3	Head Coach Larry Bird; Chris Mullin, Reggie Miller
Washington Wizards	Sun.	Feb. 15	Chris Webber & Juwan Howard
Miami Heat	Fri.	Feb. 20	Tim Hardaway, Alonzo Mourning, Pat Riley
San Antonio Spurs	Mon.	Mar. 2	David Robinson and #1 pick Tim Duncan
Detroit Pistons	Weds.	Mar. 4	Grant Hill
Portland Trail Blazers	Fri.	Mar. 27	Kenny Anderson & Arvydas Sabonis
Houston Rockets	Fri.	Apr. 10	Hakeem, Sir Charles and Clyde

Here's what you get with each 15-Game Plan:

■ **Same seat**: You get the next best seat locations, after our full season ticket holders. You'll get the same seat for each of your 15 games.

■ **FREE signing bonus**: Why not a signing bonus for fans? That's right, a signing bonus for you.

Our signing bonus to you is a little more modest than to a player. Well, maybe it's a lot more modest. Our signing bonus is really more a nice little gift of appreciation. For each 15-game plan you purchase, we'll provide you with a FREE Sacramento Kings baseball cap.

■ **Easy payment option**: If you choose, we'll divide your plan into thirds. We'll submit one-third of the cost to your credit card for three consecutive months. This will spread your payment over three months without any interest expense.

Lower level season tickets still available, call us at (916) 928-3650

15 OF THE BEST GAMES STARTING AT $180
You can get these 15 Big Games starting at $180 per plan. You'll see Michael, Sir Charles, Larry Bird, Shaq and the new Saint Jean. All great games. The best seat locations will go fast so we recommend that you order today.

Name_____
Address_____
City_____ St.____ Zip____
Phone_____
of $12 Plans_____ @ $180 ea. = _____
of $18 Plans_____ @ $270 ea. = _____
of $24 Plans_____ @ $360 ea. = _____
Payment: ❑ Check ❑ VISA ❑ MasterCard ❑ AmEx
Card No._____ Exp. Date_____
❑ Easy Payment Option

Make Check Payable to: Sacramento Kings, Attn: Game Plans, One Sports Parkway, Sacramento, CA 95834

Gary St. Jean, who had been fired the year before. The "new saint" was a rookie draft pick, Olivier St. Jean (who later changed his name to Tariq Abdul-Wahad).

Our ad was the same size as the season-ticket ad. The result:

A NEW SAINT						
Date	Medium	Ad title	Cost	Sales	Revenue	Ratio
9-11-97	*Sacramento Bee*	New Saint	$1,527	45	$55,842	$36.57
9-15-97	*Sacramento Bee*	New Saint	$1,527	11	$46,052	$30.16

We ran the New Saint ad eight times. At the end, it began to run out of steam, so we replaced it. Here are the results:

SAINT VS. TIX				
Ad title	Cost	Sales	Revenue	Ratio
Season Tix	$3,054	2	$872	$0.29
Season Tix	$12,216	360	$190,286	$15.58

When it gets down to the bottom line, would you rather get twenty-nine cents or fifteen dollars for every dollar you spend?

Here's how the New Saint ad worked.

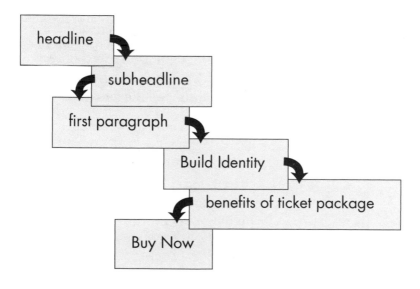

Note that one thing I was not trying to do was sell to people who weren't interested. Neither ad would entice a *Sacramento Bee* reader who was not a sports fan to buy Kings tickets. What I *was* trying to do was ferret out the reader who was interested in the Kings or basketball and provide good reasons to buy the package. To that end, I included certain items in each ad:

- Headline, to get the reader to read the subheadline.

- Subheadline, to get the reader to read the first paragraph.

- First paragraph, to get the reader to read the second paragraph.

- Interesting pictures, with captions, to help the reader get into the ad. We didn't use captions in the New Saint ad. Our mistake. If we had, the ratio might have been $40-to-$1.

- Subheads in body copy, to get the reader to read on.

- Bullet points, a good way to itemize and highlight benefits.

- Reasons for buying. Just listing the benefits isn't enough. Explain why a benefit is a good deal.

- Something free for buying. A gift is an excellent way to spur action. I offered a choice of free booklets in our trade ad for the Portland Trail Blazers.

- No reversed-out body copy. Don't let a crazed designer lay out your ad with white type on a black background. It may be more interesting graphically, but people won't read it. *Every* readership study I've seen shows that people tend to read *less* of copy that is *reversed*. So if you have really rotten copy, reverse it. Then nobody will know how rotten that copy really is.

- Price.

- Easy payment option.

- Company name, web address, address, and phone number.

- Logo — if and only if there's room.

The Fiction of Reach and Frequency

Ad agencies often measure the effectiveness of an ad campaign in terms of Reach and Frequency — that is, how much of the target audience do you reach, and how often? When you have enough ad dollars to Build Identity, that's as good a way as any, I suppose. The more people you reach, and the more often you reach them, the better chance you have to Build Identity for your brand or company. But, alas, what if you're in the position I always find myself in — not enough ad money to Build Identity? You can do what I do — throw out the measuring sticks of Reach and Frequency and use The Ratio. For every dollar we spend on an ad, how many do we get back?

When I worked on ads with pro sports teams, we always placed them on page three in the sports section of the major local newspaper. We never had enough money to run TV or radio commercials or place billboards.

"Whoa," the ad naysayer would say. "Only 35 percent of the people read that paper. You are leaving out 65 percent of the potential buyers."

"Yep," I would say. "You're right."

"So what are you going to do about it?"

"Run another ad in the newspaper," I'd say. "We simply don't have the money to reach more of our target audience more often using TV. We run our ads in the newspaper twice a week, Mondays and Thursdays."

"Not Sundays? You get a much bigger reach on Sundays."

"Yeah, but The Ratio goes down. The ads cost more on Sunday and we get less money in return." I think the ratio also goes down because there are more ads and stories competing for readers' eyeballs, and because people are more laid back on Sundays, less likely to pick up the phone and order tickets.

"Well, if you're too stubborn to think Reach, at least think Frequency," a naysayer would say.

"If we ran an ad every day, The Ratio would go down," I would reply. "Our total costs would go up, but the number of dollars coming back would not increase that much. Our newspaper ads have a shelf life of about three days. Placing an ad each of those three days doesn't increase results, it just increases costs. We live by The Ratio."

"What's this Ratio thing again?" asks the naysayer. "Some type of new measurement from the New York ad agencies?"

"The Ratio is simple. How many dollars do we get back for each dollar we spend on an ad? We can live with a $4-to-$1 ratio because we Build Identity while getting customers."

"That means you have to measure every ad!" the naysayer would exclaim.

"Yep. If you can't measure response, why spend money to run the ad?"

The naysayer would pause and think. Then he would say, "If you run ads to Build Identity, you can't measure that."

"I agree with you," I'd reply.

"You do?"

"Yep, if you run ads only to Build Identity, you've got a lot of cute little ads, but they're very difficult to measure. Then you have to hire a research company to ask people how they liked your ads. However, if you ask the ad to Build Identity *and* Buy Now, then it's easy to measure."

"That sounds un-American," the naysayer would say. "As advertising professionals, we must preserve the right to spend a lot of money on advertising without knowing the results."

Big Ad Budgets in Heaven

The teams and companies I've worked with have always had limited ad budgets. That's probably warped my thinking about advertising. Maybe there are big ad budgets in heaven. Maybe I'll be able to measure things by Reach and Frequency and cost per thousand and cost per point instead of The Ratio. Maybe The Ratio is just a worldly thing with no applications in heaven. That would be terrific. Just spend, spend, spend.

I wonder if that's any fun?

A SIMPLE TEST YOU CAN TAKE

1. The Rubber Chicken theory also works for brochures. (True/False)

2. How do you know when it's time to change ads?
   a. When you get tired of seeing it.
   b. When your prospects tell you to stop.

3. Which item doesn't fit in a good ad?
   a. Headline.
   b. Picture.
   c. Hype.
   d. An overwhelming negative about the product.
   e. Lots of copy.

Answers

1. True. The Rubber Chicken works for any type of communication. The first rule is to catch a prospect's attention

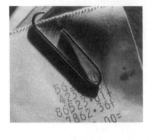

— whether with a headline, a picture, a rubber chicken, or three dollars.

Three dollars? We used that to help the San Francisco Giants market suites in their planned downtown China Basin ballpark. The Giants had some fancy, expensive brochures, but if the right person at a company didn't see them, there was no sale. We wanted to put the brochure into prospects' hands *after* they had come to see the Giants' mock suite. The trick, of course, was to get prospects to trek over to the China Basin office.

I suggested to Tom McDonald, executive VP of the China Basin Ballpark Company, that he send a letter to the CEOs of all companies within walking distance of the ballpark. To make sure the secretary passed the letter along and the CEO read it, we paper-clipped three dollars to it.

Here's how the letter began:

> Dear Joe:
> You and I are neighbors.
> That and $3.00 will get you a cup of coffee today.
> Instead of spending the money at Starbucks, however, I've got a better idea. Even though you and I haven't met, I'd like you to have a cup of coffee with me at my office.
> There's one good reason for that.
> I've got something that our neighborhood has been waiting for for 30 years. Major league baseball.
> Downtown.
> Does this help you in your business? I've got proof that it will. Undeniably.

We followed up this letter with a phone call to set up an appointment.

When the CEO visited the mock suite, we usually made the sale. Then we'd hand over our nifty brochure.

At the time, the Giants were frozen at $20 million in suite and seat license sales. If they didn't reach $70 million, the ballpark wouldn't be built. With the help of $3 here and $3 there, the Giants quickly flew past the $70 million mark.

2. b. When your prospects tell you to stop. They tell you to stop by not responding to the ad. Then what do you do? Run a different ad. At the New Jersey Nets, we once ran the same ad seventeen straight times. We got bored with it, but it kept on pulling. As long as it made The Ratio, we kept running the ad. When it fell below $4-to-$1, we ran a new ad.

Remember, these ads aren't just to Build Identity; you also need to get The Ratio. When an ad doesn't reach The Ratio the first time it is run, it won't reach it the second or third time. There is no cumulative benefit. Replace it immediately.

3. c. Hype. Advertising is supposed to be hype, right? Well, maybe in those Build Identity TV commercials. But with Rubber Chicken advertising, hype doesn't work. Instead, it casts doubt on the product's credibility. In Rubber Chicken advertising, you get prospects interested, then give them good reasons to buy.

If the product has an overwhelming negative, it's better to write about it up front than sweep it under the carpet. The Sacramento Kings, who owned their arena, bought an indoor soccer team, the Knights, to bring in revenue in the summer. However, indoor soccer isn't the NBA, and tickets proved hard to sell. The Kings' solution? Give them away, and make money on parking, hot dogs, beer, etc.

They gave away thousands of tickets. Tens of thousands. Every man, woman, and child in the Sacramento area probably received free tickets at one time or another. But as the Kings gave away more and more Knights tickets, the few people who still bought them stopped buying.

This seemed an impossible situation. The ticket revenue was essential for survival. The general manager of the Knights asked me to help.

We decided to feature the overwhelming negative — the tens of thousands of free tickets — in a one-eighth page ad:

(Headline) Better Than Free

(Subheadline) We've discounted tickets in the past. This is something that you won't mind paying for.

(First paragraph) You may have gone to one of our games on a free ticket. The free ticket could have come from a friend. Or from us.

(Second paragraph) Once you were at the game, the cost of the ticket didn't matter. What did count was that you had fun. You noticed right away that our game is fast paced. It's exciting. It's high scoring.

(Third paragraph) If you have come to one of our games on a free or discounted ticket, we've got a better deal for you. This is a better deal even if you have to pay for it. Fat chance, you may say, but read on.

(Fourth paragraph) We start by giving you a free gift. It's a $70 genuine game ball.

Can you see the slippery slide? The offer, by the way, was that anyone buying two $35 ticket packages got five weekend games and a $70 genuine game ball.

The ticket price in the package wasn't discounted. It remained $7. This was the first time in years the Knights had charged full price. The game ball? It cost the Knights less than $5. In effect, we took the normal $1 discount and used it to buy a soccer ball that added value to the package.

What were the results? A $3-to-$1 ratio — a little less than we'd like, but a whole lot better than $0-to-$1.

CHAPTER 13

Two Rules to Forget

Some time ago I had my own company that sold products to big consumer product firms like Gillette, Anheuser-Busch, and Procter & Gamble. I figured the best way to sell my products in each case was to call on the company president.

Getting an appointment was a skill in itself, but to make it pay off I had to do one other thing: research. I had to find out everything I could about the person and the company I was going to approach.

Today, the Internet makes this kind of research easy. At the time, though, it meant digging through the library. That's why I hired two Northwestern University students as part-time researchers. Their job was simple: comb through the periodical files and make a copy of every article published in the past two years about the company. I paid by the piece.

This usually produced a stack of copies three or four inches high. I would read through the articles, set them aside for a day, then read them again. I knew that sometime during the meeting I would need 1 percent of that information. I just didn't know which 1 percent. So I got familiar with 100 percent of it.

One of my target companies was Gillette. I picked up the phone and made an appointment with the company president, Ed Gelsthorpe, also known as "Cranapple Ed." Ed had become president of Ocean Spray Cranberries in 1959. Just before Thanksgiving, there was a nationwide panic about a pesticide that had contaminated a few batches of cranberries. Nobody was injured, and the panic quickly subsided, but Ocean Spray took a big hit. Ed responded by coming up with "Cranapple Juice." It became a year-round favorite, and the company prospered.

My meeting with Ed was delightful, and I walked away with a nice piece of business. But the thing that has stuck with me to this day was a story that was less than 1 percent of the stack of articles, and not the 1 percent I used to make the sale. It was a story about King Gillette, founder of the Gillette Company.

Around 1900, King Gillette was a traveling salesman. One morning on the road in the Midwest, King dropped his straight razor. It broke in half. If you've done much traveling, you know this kind of aggravation is typical. That broken razor, however, gave King an idea. He glued the two pieces back to back, thus giving his single-blade straight razor two sharp edges. He sent a telegram to his wife. It said, "Forget all of our problems. We're rich!"

When he got back to Boston a month or so later, he found a company that could make him a prototype of this two-sided razor. Then he went out to sell it.

The first year he sold three.

The next year he sold seven.

He became obsessed about this crazy two-sided razor.

The following year he sold eleven.

It went like that for a few years. His obsession didn't abate.

His friends would mock him: "Hey, King, how's your razor doing?" Heh, heh, haw, haw.

Then King Gillette did something really outrageous in marketing. He gave his razors away for free.

World War I had broken out. Gillette took the train to Washington. He offered the army his razor, free. Great patriotic gesture. The army loved free things. The razor was portable, and you didn't need a strap to sharpen it. When the blade got dull, you just inserted a new blade — a blade bought from the fledgling Gillette Safety Razor Company.

His sales jumped to over 1 million blades that year.

Heh, heh, haw, haw.

When Sponsors Ruled

Gillette owned Friday night TV in the 1950s. The *Gillette Cavalcade of Sports* featured boxing matches and the World Series. Competitors did not even think of trying to buy into those shows. They were Gillette's alone.

About the same time, Hallmark Cards owned a program called *Playhouse 90*. Texaco owned the biggest audience, with comedian Milton Berle.

It took less than twenty years, but all that "owning" of programs disappeared. It got too expensive, they say.

It may have been expensive, but just as important was the proliferation of media. When Gillette and Hallmark and Kraft dominated, there were only three networks. Then independent TV stations started to pop up all over the place. Then cable. Then satellite. With cable

and satellite nowadays, you can choose from over 300 channels. It's pretty tough to dominate one channel, let alone
three hundred.

Advertising underwent a major shift in strategy; the new
mantra was Reach and Frequency. This change was the real
reason big companies lost their dominance of television
programs. As title sponsorship became more expensive, ad
agencies developed Reach and Frequency criteria.

If you were Gillette, you dominated the male viewing
audience with your Friday night fights. What about the rest
of the week? Uh-oh. No dominance there. No Reach. No
Frequency.

To get that Reach and Frequency, Gillette gave up its
domination. So did Texaco. So did Kraft. So did Hallmark. It
was the end of domination.

Reach and Frequency vs. Plastic Man

Reach and Frequency can work for you if you have the
following:

1. **A monster ad budget.** If you're Coca-Cola and have
more ad dollars than you know what to do with, then Reach
and Frequency is a perfect way to spend that fortune. Go
ahead, buy everything the TV networks offer; buy commercials on at least 70 percent of the radio stations in a market.
Buy frequently and buy often. Oops, you still have money
left over? Increase your frequency even more.

2. **A monster ad budget.** That's right; there is no other
reason. If you don't have Coca-Cola's budget, then read on.
You'll find you don't really need it. You can spend some of
that fortune somewhere else and keep the rest as profit.

About the time Gillette was sponsoring the Friday night fights, there was a comic-book hero named Plastic Man — a sort of superhero Gumby who could stretch himself into wild contortions to save the day. Well, if you apply the thinking of Marketing Outrageously to electronic media, it's like having Plastic Man perform a full and astounding stretch on your ad dollars.

The first part of this stretch, however, is that you have to toss out the rules of Reach and Frequency. If you're reluctant, then just set them aside for the moment; I wouldn't want you to hyperventilate.

Instead of referring to the Reach and Frequency numbers your ad agency computes, try this: rank the radio stations and TV shows that best fit your demographics. For instance, if you could advertise on just one radio station in your market, which one would it be?

1. What radio station best fits my demographics?

2. What radio station is second best for my demographics?

3. Finally, what radio station is third best for my demographics?

That's all for radio. Now do the same exercise for TV shows on either your local channels, or cable and satellite.

1. What is the TV show that best fits my demographics?

2. What TV show is second best for my demographics?

3. What TV show is third best for my demographics?

Now ask yourself, and your ad agency, "What's it going to take to dominate that first radio station or that first show?"

Your ad agency might ask, "Uh, what do you mean, 'dominate'?"

You might want to use the *Gillette Cavalcade of Sports* as an example, but that level of domination is difficult to achieve today. The purpose of domination, however, is the same — to persuade listeners or viewers to buy your product.

Here's an example: The ad agency for a minor-league baseball team I was working with designed a Reach and Frequency plan for a radio and TV ad campaign. It was pretty impressive, with charts and everything. The commercials would have reached 86 percent of the market about four times each.

I asked the ad agency to list the three most important radio stations and the three most important TV shows. Then I asked The Question: "What's it going to take to dominate the first radio station on the list and the first TV show?"

"The team *could* dominate one of those stations or one of those shows," they said, "but it would cut your reach way, way down."

I said, "I know, but humor me."

Their number-one TV pick was ESPN's *SportsCenter.* However, they had originally recommended a "scatter plan" that covered *SportsCenter* and a lot of other programs. In the revised, "What's it going to take?" thinking, the team would buy two 30-second commercials each time *SportsCenter* aired, for a month. If *SportsCenter* ran four times a day, the baseball team would run eight 30-second commercials a day. This pretty much eliminated the other TV shows.

"That's a bit outrageous," the ad agency said. "You've knocked your reach way down. Nobody but viewers of *SportsCenter* will even know about the team."

"That's okay," I said.

Here's why it's okay.

1. **What's it going to take to persuade somebody to buy?** It's going to take running the same commercial to the same people a lot of times. Four or five times in a month is not

enough. Sure, it might make people a little bit aware of the product, but it's not enough to get them to buy. You need to reach the same audience twelve to fifteen times or more each week. Thirty times a week would even be better.

2. **You're in the top two in consumers' minds.** Consumers don't think in terms of market share; they think about which brands are socially acceptable for them to buy. If your favorite toothpaste is out of stock at the store, you don't look at all the other brands on the shelf. You pick one that has somehow etched itself into your brain, making it socially acceptable to use. When you dominate a TV program and dominate it regularly, you imprint your product on the minds of its viewers as socially acceptable to buy and use.

Is it enough to be number two in their minds? If you have dozens of competitors, you've outperformed all but one. You can make a fortune as number one or number two in consumers' minds, even if you're fifteenth in market share. Remember, consumers don't think in terms of market share; they recognize two brands per category. By consistently dominating a TV show, you become one of those brands.

Yes, if you subscribe to Reach and Frequency theory, you should reach more people. Unfortunately, it would be less frequently. More people would be aware of your product, but would they be persuaded to buy it?

3. **Viewers have friends, too.** When your advertising convinces one person that your brand is socially acceptable, chances are that person will pass the message along to a friend. It's called "buy and tell."

In any market that has a pro baseball team, only about 5 percent of the population will buy a ticket in a given season. If your ad budget for ticket sales is based on Reach and Frequency, it will probably reach the 95 percent who will not buy a ticket. Sure, they will be aware of your team, but they still won't buy tickets. If, however, you aim at dominating sports-oriented TV shows, you'll probably be etching your message into the brains of fans who will at least consider buying a ticket. If you can persuade them to buy tickets more frequently, they will become missionaries who will bring their friends into your fold.

The Ratio Still Rules

I've already confessed my small-budget bias: I believe each ad dollar should be accountable in terms of sales. In print advertising, returns are easy to track. You run an ad, hang around the phone, and write the orders. After a few days, you add up all the money you got and stack it against the cost of the ad. Your goal: $4-to-$1.

With electronic media — radio, TV, and the Internet — I still say if the ads don't bring in sales, don't run the ads. It

 takes a little longer to measure sales because you have to run a series of commercials over several weeks. But if you truly dominate a TV or radio show, the results will come much more quickly and you will be able to *feel* it.

The Corcoran Group, a Manhattan real estate company, proved this. Their advertising dominated one channel — financial news cable channel CNBC. The Corcoran Group ran the same thirty-second commercial up to eleven times a day. The commercial featured the 1951 Rosemary Clooney hit song "Come on-a My House."

"If you pull the ad, I'll give you stock tips for a week," said one of the many traders on Wall Street, as reported in the *Wall Street Journal.*

"I'm hearing that song in my sleep," said another. "The ad's got a cult following on Wall Street."

Obviously, the Corcoran Group didn't follow the rules of Reach and Frequency. They set out to dominate just one channel. Although the ad might have started to grate on viewers, the results were outstanding; web traffic to their site jumped 70 percent.

Your Hit Parade

If you haven't tossed out the Reach and Frequency philosophy yet, do it now. See, you didn't hyperventilate. Now list the radio stations and TV shows that best fit your demographics.

Radio Stations   TV Shows

1. _____   1. _____

2. _____   2. _____

3. _____   3. _____

Now ask yourself, "What's it going to take to dominate the first station on the list?"

Write down the number of commercials it will take to dominate. Look at the station's rate card; suppose it costs too much to dominate. Then ask yourself another question: "What's it going to take to dominate a

segment of that radio station?" You might have enough in your ad budget to dominate morning drivetime, or you might have to settle for the less expensive late-night hours. That's okay. Just dominate!

Let's say your math shows you can dominate your top-choice TV show and still have money left in your budget. Ask yourself another question: "What's it going to take to dominate the second show on my list?"

Still have money left? Well, you know the next question. And if there's still money left after dominating the third show or station, don't ask yourself any more questions. Reduce your ad budget. Put the extra money into bonuses or into the profit column. That profit column, by the way, will get even bigger, because you're persuading more and more people to become your customers.

Now, how outrageous is that?

A SIMPLE TEST YOU CAN TAKE

1. Consumers think market share when buying a product. (True/False)

2. You can have great Reach and Frequency stats and not sell anything. (True/False)

Answers

1. False. Many consumers have never even heard the words "market" and "share" used together. They just buy whatever is socially acceptable. If your product or company is already socially acceptable, you've got to keep advertising so others won't elbow you aside and take your place. If it's not, you'll have to do something outrageous to hurl yourself in. That's what RC Cola did in Dayton, Ohio in 2000.

As you know, Coca-Cola and Pepsi have a lock on the world soft-drink market. They have the beachfront-property shelf space in the supermarkets and enough money to fend off would-be invaders. Except in Dayton, Ohio, where RC Cola beat Coca-Cola and Pepsi to become the dominating sponsor of the Dayton Dragons, a minor-league baseball team.

Big deal, you say. It's minor-league baseball. But let's take a closer look.

There are no major-league teams in Dayton. Then Dayton built a beautiful downtown ballpark. The fans fell in love with their team. So did RC Cola.

That love affair brought them two important things:

- **Exclusivity in the ballpark.** If you want a soft drink in the ballpark, you can't get a Coke or a Pepsi, but you can have anything RC distributes. Over 600,000 people per season attend a Dayton Dragons game. That's 600,000 potential samplers of RC Cola, 7-UP, Diet-Rite, and Snapple who will not be distracted by Coke or Pepsi. Many of them will find that RC's drinks are pretty good, and therefore socially acceptable to them. RC Cola can't become Dayton's market leader — Coke and Pepsi are just too formidable — but RC can capture some of the giants' market share.

- **Dominant identity.** Dayton's downtown ballpark is the centerpiece of the market. It is more important to Dayton than Madison Square Garden is to New York City. Inside the stadium, RC Cola dominates. There are no Coke or Pepsi signs to muddle up RC's identity. RC has the longest fence sign in the history of fence signs — 250 feet long, running from the right-field foul pole to center field, then picking up in left field. If you walked into the stadium for the first time and were asked, "Name just one advertiser and you win $100," you'd say, "RC Cola, gimme the hundred." It's that dominating.

Being socially acceptable and locally dominant pays off in the supermarket. In the Dayton Dragons' first season, RC set a sales record in June, broke that record in July, and broke it again in August. And this was in a soda market without fizz because of rising competition from bottled water and fruit drinks. Total Dayton-area soft drink sales fell 4 percent, but RC went up 4 percent. Pretty good for someone not Coke and not Pepsi.

Alas, the tale doesn't end here. Let's jump forward to mergers and acquisitions. On a national basis, RC Cola and its other brands became involved in a series of mergers and acquistions. Someplace along the line, they let their sponsorship with the Dayton Dragons lapse. Guess who jumped in? Right you are: Coca-Cola. Guess what happened to RC's market share? Right you are: it dropped.

2. True. Marketers obsessed with Reach and Frequency math are focusing on the wrong thing. They should be thinking: What's it going to take to persuade the consumer to buy my product? Answer: The advertising has to make an impact. An easy way to make an impact is to dominate a radio station or TV show.

An impressive Reach and Frequency number, used as a sales tool within the trade, might help boost distribution. That alone will help sales. However, Reach and Frequency doesn't make products fly off the shelves. You still have to persuade people to buy. To do that, you have to cut through the clutter and talk to some of the consumers time after time after time.

CHAPTER 14

Differentiate Until You Sweat

Two weeks in Ireland: golf in the morning, writing in the afternoon, a few pints of Guinness at night. That was my regimen shortly after leaving the New Jersey Nets.

The writing produced the first few chapters of *Ice to the Eskimos*.

The golf produced a lot of fun and some interesting anecdotes.

The Guinness produced an idea that scared the pants off a Budweiser executive.

The idea was born in an Irish pub. I was savoring a Guinness, thinking how much better this famous Irish brew was than ordinary beer, and a thought occurred to me. I asked the bartender, "What's the second-best-selling beer in Ireland?"

"Guinness," said the bartender.

I was shocked. I'd figured Guinness for a 90 percent market share.

"What in the world is number one?" I asked.

"Budweiser."

"Budweiser's the top-selling beer in Ireland?"

"It sure is," the bartender said. "All the younger lads love it."

"Does Anheuser-Busch have a brewery in Ireland?" I asked.

"Nope. Guinness brews it. Here, let me give you a taste." He poured half a pint of Budweiser into a glass and set it in front of me.

It didn't taste like the Budweiser back home. It seemed silkier, smoother, better. A lot better.

That's when the idea hit me. Why not import Budweiser from Ireland? Call it "Bud from Ireland." Charge a premium price.

The thought lay dormant for a few months. Then, while giving a speech back in the United States, I half-joked about my "Bud from Ireland" idea.

Afterwards, a guy came over to me at the bar and introduced himself. He was a big-shot executive from Anheuser-Busch, and he was on the warpath.

"You can't do that — that Bud from Ireland thing," he said.

"Why?" I asked, surprised at his vehement reaction.

"The Budweiser from Ireland tastes a lot better than our regular Budweiser," he said. "Plus, you'd have a special marketing cachet that would make Bud from Ireland cool and hip. The younger beer drinkers might fall in love with it."

"Yes, and . . . ?"

"Anyway, I don't think Guinness's license with us would let them import it," he added nervously. "I'll have to check."

"Why don't you guys do it yourself?" I asked. "Just give me a lifetime supply of free Bud from Ireland for bringing you the idea."

"Nah, Bud from Ireland would always be compared with regular Budweiser. It's better just to leave it over there."

I sipped my Budweiser and thought about that for a minute. Anheuser-Busch had gambled millions of dollars marketing specialty labels like Bud Dry and Bud Ice, none of which had carved out a profitable niche. They had siphoned off a few Bud customers, but none from Miller or Coors or the imports.

But what if Bud from Ireland became a popular *import?* Because of the price, it wouldn't cannibalize regular Bud, but it might take large bites out of Heineken, the leading import. It might even become the top import.

Since Anheuser-Busch didn't offer me a lifetime supply of free Bud from Ireland, I guess I'll just have to buy my own.

I'll drink to that.

BREW IT YOURSELF

If you consider my idea about Bud from Ireland a little outrageous, think about this: Let's you and I start our own domestic brewery.

It won't cost billions (or even millions) of dollars to get started. Just two things: a little moxie, and a lot of outrageous marketing.

The reason it won't cost millions is that we won't build a brewery like the big sudsers. We won't even build a microbrewery — those room-size kettles cost a lot of money. Instead, we'll let someone else do the brewing. You and I will concentrate on Marketing Outrageously.

That's what a guy named Jim Koch (pronounced "Cook") did. In 1984, Koch created, from scratch, the Boston Beer Company. His brand: Samuel Adams.

What did Koch do that was so outrageous?

- **He didn't brew his own beer.** Although the identity of Samuel Adams beer is steeped in New England lore, the beer was first brewed in Pennsylvania by Pittsburgh Brewing, producer of Iron City Beer. Bud and Miller were slowly swiping market share from Iron City, so Pittsburgh Brewing had plenty of capacity to brew a private label like Samuel Adams.

- **He priced his beer higher than the imports** — about 15 percent over Heineken. After all, if it's priced higher, it must have higher quality hops and grains and stuff, right?

- With this pricing strategy, Koch was clearly not putting Budweiser or Miller into the crosshairs. Good thinking. They'd just chew up his gun — crosshairs and all — and then munch on Boston Beer. Koch's targets were Heineken and the other imports. He would lure the premium beer buyer, the one for whom price isn't the foremost object. With his low overhead, Koch could also offer bars and restaurants contracts with bigger profit margins.

- **He didn't sponsor sports on TV.** Going toe-to-toe with the big guys would have meant spending his way into oblivion. Instead, Koch bought magazine ads telling the legend of Samuel Adams, brewer and patriot. Actually, the brewer part was a bit of a stretch; Adams owned a malt mill but ran it into the ground. But he is credited with the outrageous idea of dumping all that tea from England into Boston Harbor, otherwise known as the Boston Tea Party.

- **He exported his beer to Germany.** Not that Germany is a high-profit export market — Koch just wanted to say in his ads, "The only American beer exported to Germany."

- **He won the Denver Beerfest.** Other breweries have won taste competitions with little fanfare, but Koch trumpeted his award as if it were the Nobel Prize.

Though competitors accused Koch of rigging the vote, the win gave another justification for Samuel Adams to charge a higher price.

- **He championed smallness.** "I brew in a year what the largest-selling import makes in just three hours," said one ad, "because I take the time to brew Samuel Adams right." In other words, Samuel Adams was brewed with more care, more craftsmanship than the mass-produced competition. Not mentioned, of course, was the fact that Pittsburgh Brew-ing was the brewmaster, nor that Pittsburgh Brewing could have brewed a lot more Samuel Adams if there were more sales.

Each of the points above could be considered a little bit outrageous.

- **Not brew your own beer?** Outrageous.

- **Price it higher than the imports?** Outrageous.

- **Don't spend big on TV?** Outrageous.

- **Export to Germany?** Outrageous.

- **Win a taste competition?** Who cares?

- **Be smaller and better and more caring?** Good point. I like that one. That really sounds good.

With a limited marketing and advertising budget, Samuel Adams shrewdly differentiated itself from its competitors simply by being outrageous. The big breweries spent fortunes trying to differentiate themselves, but all their slick Reach and Frequency commercials just blended into one big burp.

The Great Wall of Ohio

Differentiation is not just for beer or other consumer products. I've consulted for pro sports teams, Internet companies, and a wide variety of other businesses. It doesn't matter to me whether the industry involves cans or cars, paper or peanut butter, round balls, pointed balls, or pucks. To me, business is business, and Marketing Outrageously is Marketing Outrageously. The one thing I look for in every marketing job is how to *differentiate the company*.

There are guidelines, of course. You could differentiate a company by having everyone go naked. "Oh yeah," others would say, "those are the fools who wear no clothes." But would it bring in staggering amounts of revenue? Probably not. Differentiation should be innovative, but socially acceptable; bold, but not reckless; daring, but not foolish.

In mid-1999, I got a call from Mandalay Pictures, makers of movies and owners of two minor-league baseball teams. They were starting a new team in Ohio, and they wanted me as a consultant. So I went to Dayton and started thinking about how to differentiate the Dayton Dragons.

This is the image of a minor-league baseball team:

- **No-name players.** Except for the time Michael Jordan left basketball and played for the Birmingham Barons in the '90s, there are no superstars in the minor leagues. Budding stars, maybe, but these usually play just one season before moving up the ladder. In fact, most minor-league teams don't know who they've got until just days before the first game.

- **Cheap tickets.** Tickets to a major-league game in any sport cost lots of money, but you can still see a minor-league baseball game for less than the price of a movie. Minor-league sports are terrific family entertainment.

- **Outfield fence signs.** An important revenue source for minor-league baseball teams is advertising signs on their outfield fence. Many teams sell upwards of seventy 4-by-8 foot spots on outfield walls. In many cases, this small sign is a way that the sponsor supports the local team — sort of a charitable contribution.

    In Dayton, we decided to offer prospective advertisers something different on the most valuable ad real estate, the outfield fence. Instead of being one of seventy or eighty postage stamps, a company's ad would cover 250 feet of the outfield wall.  (If you have trouble visualizing 250 feet, think football for a moment. Two hundred fifty feet represents a little more than 80 yards on the football field.) And it would move! We bought LED electronic sign equipment like the replay boards you see in almost every arena and stadium. (Until the Dallas Cowboys built their new stadium in 2009, the Dayton LED outfield wall was the longest LED sign in sports.)

    At the push of a button, we could change the whole sign. Each of seven sponsors would rotate across the world's longest outfield fence sign.

    We showed our salespeople how to drive home the point when visiting prospective sponsors. "Could you walk with me for a minute?" says the Dragons' salesperson to the prospect.

"Well — okay," says the prospect. "Where are we going?"

"Just remember where we started," the salesperson says. That's pretty easy; they're starting at the prospect's office. They walk out through a maze of cubicles, out the door, across the street, into a parking lot.

"Remember where we started?" the salesperson asks.

The prospect nods.

"That's where your fence sign would start. It would stretch all the way out to here."

We "burned in" this image with a large fold-out page in the proposal — a tight illustration of the stadium, with the prospect's company logo repeated over the entire length of the 250-foot fence sign.

The reception was terrific. Our monster sign differentiated us in sponsors' minds. They looked upon us as marketers who could help them, not just a minor-league ball club looking for a donation.

Was it more expensive for the sponsors? You'd better believe it. A lot more expensive. By being innovative, bold, and daring, we got triple the usual advertising revenue for the same fence real estate. By cutting the number of sponsors from seventy to seven, we reduced our visual clutter. And, the sponsor was able to truly dominate in the ballpark.

Branding Can Be a Four-Letter Word

If you looked on Amazon.com right now for a book on *branding*, you could choose among 2,522 books. If you wait a month, there might be 100 more. I've read six or seven, so I only have 2,515 to go.

I think the sole purpose of branding is to differentiate your product or company from its competitors. But I stop talking about branding when it starts to cost a lot of money. Many so-called branding efforts cost a fortune.

Now don't get me wrong. I think the branding that Nike has done is terrific and fun. Nike has taken gym shoes, spent a few billion dollars in edgy ads, and turned its shoes and clothing into *lifestyle* products.

I think the branding that Budweiser does is fantastic. Think of the fun we could have in producing nonsensical thirty-second commercials for Bud Light! Or a cool commercial featuring the Clydesdales tromping through snow. These commercials helped Budweiser achieve a market share of over 50 percent! So, long live branding. (As long as you have billions of ad dollars!)

What about the rest of us that don't have a few extra billion (or millions or even thousands) to spend on branding?

Well, I've got two laws on branding for folks that don't have billions in an ad budget. Here's my first law on Outrageous Branding:

1. **Branding begins and ends with your current customer.** *Begins* and *ends* are the operative words. Forget about your prospective customers. For the moment, only think of your current customers.

Now the second law of Outrageous Branding:

2. **Get your current customers to say nice things about you.** That's the subject that we would spend a couple of days' worth of meetings on every year with our baseball teams at Mandalay Baseball Properties.

But let's take another business. How about garbage collection? If you were in that business, how would you brand *garbage*?

Let's look at a garbage company (others call it *waste management*) in Oregon. This waste management (gar-

bage) company's name is Western Oregon Waste. Or W.O.W. That's right, WOW. That's what they have plastered on the sides of their garbage trucks — WOW.

If you lived in WOW's marketing area, the company would collect your garbage every week. If you went to its website, www.westernoregonwaste.com, you could do the traditional things like paying your bill. But there's also a downloadable comic book that in a clear and fun way describes all of WOW's services. (If you're currently a customer, you received the WOW comic book with one of your billings.)

Here's just a few of the services you'll find in the comic book:

- Extra garbage pick-up.

- Clean up your garage and you don't lift a finger.

- Pick up old appliances.

- Pick up and dispose of hazardous wastes.

- Spread bark dust where you want it on your lawn.

Heck, if you lived in WOW's marketing area and paged through their comic book, you'd see about seven to ten new ways of spending your money with them.

So, WOW is not Nike, it's not McDonald's, it's not a baseball team, *it's a garbage company*. Er, waste management company.

Let's see how they spent their so-called branding budget.

1. **Painted trucks**. They painted WOW and Western Oregon Waste on the sides of their trucks. Wouldn't they have painted their trucks anyway? They just made their trucks *interesting*. WOW!

2. **Website**. They would have had a website anyway, right? They just made it entertaining with their comic book motif. WOW!

3. **Comic books**. They would have done some type of brochure about their services, right? Do you cringe at the thought of a traditional brochure about garbage? It would have been uninteresting, boring, and unread. As a comic book, however, their brochure was actually *fun* to read. It covered everything you would ever need to know about garbage, and you enjoyed the time you spent becoming so knowledgeable. WOW!

Western Oregon Waste is a fun company. And, they're a garbage company. Walk around McMinnville, Astoria, or Seaside and ask folks about WOW. The people that you ask (WOW's current customers) will say a lot of nice things about them.

Does that branding and having nice things said about WOW make any difference? Well, about 10 percent of a typical waste management company's revenue comes from extra services. At WOW it's twice that amount. That extra 10 percent is a lot more fun than the 1.5 percent boost that the airlines get for gouging their customers.

A CHEAP WAY TO DIFFERENTIATE

Remember the Southwest Airlines "bags fly free" story in chapter 7? What part of your business represents charging for checked suitcases? There's probably something in your business that rankles, or somewhat rankles, your customers. Identify it.

With a sports team, it's often women's restrooms at ballparks. Nah, we don't charge women to go into the restrooms, but I've been told that it is not a delightful experience visiting a women's restroom at a ballpark.

We changed that with our Frisco RoughRiders team. We hired a woman who designs display windows for stores. We told her we had hardly any money for this project. In fact, we asked her if she liked baseball. After all, tickets to baseball games were her payment for her ideas. We paid for the paint and other stuff.

The women's restrooms started off clean. That was good. But they were sorta "prison gray." Our consultant had them

painted sunny pastel colors. She placed knickknacks on the walls. She hung mobiles from the ceiling. She added a shelf where we could put fresh-cut flowers before every game. The restroom was still a restroom, but it was now more of a pleasant experience.

The *Dallas Morning News* ran a full-page pictorial article about our new restrooms. The TV stations ran stories on the nightly news. And we placed a prominent link on our website *featuring our bathrooms*. We had to be the only team in sports to feature our restrooms on our website.

The cost of this differentiation was less than $5,000.

(By the way, when Major League Baseball took control of the websites of minor-league teams, they didn't think it was appropriate to feature restrooms on the team's website. I guess naysayers are everywhere. I still think, however, that every team should make the women's restrooms a priority.)

Yep, "bags fly free" and delightful women's restrooms are two cool ways to differentiate.

An Outrageous Habit

When I begin working with a new client, I reflexively start thinking of ways the company could differentiate itself. It's become a habit, a little game I play. After I get to know the company better, I may mention some of these ideas. The usual reply? "That's a little outrageous for us. Our manage-ment team wouldn't go for it."

That's probably what the naysay-ers said to Jim Koch when he talked about Samuel Adams beer.

Or to the brave president of Aflac who chose to use a duck for his conservative insurance company.

Or to the Dayton Dragons when they decided to create the longest outfield fence sign in the history of the world.

Southwest probably just laughed and said, "What the heck is a naysayer anyway?"

A SIMPLE TEST YOU CAN TAKE

1. Write down one idea where you think you could dif-ferentiate your company. Don't worry about getting the idea approved. Just write down the idea.

_____

_____

_____

_____

2. How do you get these ideas approved?
   a. Own the company.
   b. Build an altar in your bedroom and make
      perpetual novenas for a year.
   c. Keep reading.

Answers

1. The idea could be as silly as Samuel Adams beer becoming the only American beer to be imported into Germany. The point is that once you start thinking about how to differentiate your company, it's pretty easy to come up with ideas. So get out a yellow pad and start writing.

2. c. This is another matter altogether, and it's a question I get every time I give a speech. I've got a sure-fire way. (Keep reading — and if you want to see this subject covered at greater length, read my previous book, *Ice to the Eskimos*.)

The reason a typical outrageous idea dies is because the idea person is unprepared to defend it. Let's say you go to see the boss with a great but outrageous proposal. You say, "Hey, here's a great idea. What if we . . ." The boss says, "You mean, give up all the revenue we get from . . ." You, unprepared for this objection, stutter, "Well, yes, I suppose that would happen, but we could probably work that out later . . ." Boss says, "Forget it. If it could work, somebody would already have done it."

You retreat to your office, and ten minutes later, the answer to his objection pops into your head. But now it's too late to go running down the hall screaming, "I've got it!"

Instead of treating a new idea as an opportunity to engage the boss in a creative discussion, you've got to go in armed to the teeth with a complete, solid, workable proposal. You're not floating a trial balloon; you're going in to get the idea *accepted.* No matter how outrageous it may seem at first, no matter how many objections the boss could raise, you've got the answers the first time you broach the subject.

Your Proposal on Paper

First, prepare yourself in writing. Build a five- to ten-page document — an executive summary — that fully outlines, details, and supports your proposal. This document should be well thought out, rational, factual, unemotional, and rock-solid. It will serve as the basis for your oral presentation and will help you prepare for this. It will also be left for the decision maker to read — but only after you've finished your oral presentation.

The written proposal should include (1) the foreword, in which you accurately and fairly describe the current situation or problem; (2) the concept, a one- or two-paragraph statement of your idea for addressing the situation; (3) the rationale, the reasons the company should implement the idea, including a cash-flow analysis; (4) the problems, or possible downsides to the idea, in which you fully confront the objections you're likely to get to your idea; and (5) the summary, one or two paragraphs calling for approval and giving a timetable.

A word of warning: Watch the hype! A proposal that's full of hype can damage your credibility. Go through the document and delete every wildly assertive statement. Eliminate adjectives and adverbs that aren't strictly essential. You can afford to exaggerate a bit in your oral presentation, but not in this document, which puts you on record.

Your Oral Presentation

When you go in to present and defend your idea in person, make it known that you have it all down in writing — but don't hand over the document just yet. You don't want them tuning you out and thumbing ahead to your colorful pie charts. The fact that you have documents to present gives you credibility: this isn't just idle daydreaming, it's a serious, well-thought-out proposal. However, a little exaggeration or hype is okay in your oral presentation, as long as you don't misrepresent the facts. Remember, the written record of your presentation will be in their hands after you leave.

Begin by stating your foreword. Don't read it aloud; just say it in plain words, as if it came up in conversation. Then lead your audience smoothly into the second part of the proposal, the concept. It's quite simple: A, here's the problem, B, here's a quick outline of my solution. If you state the problem accurately and outline a plausible solution, you'll have your listeners on the verge of being hooked.

But objections will be raised; you can be sure of it. Naysayers work on instinct. They'll spot the weaknesses right away and go for your throat. That's when you need to stay in control of your presentation. If necessary, say something to give yourself a little breathing room — for example, "I'll answer that question in a minute, but first let me finish describing this idea."

When you start talking numbers, it's a good idea to open your report, read the numbers out loud, and hold your tables and charts where they can be seen. If your figures are reasonable, your presentation will go smoothly.

Now it's time to wrap it up. Summarize your proposal, present the booklet to your listeners, and suggest a date to get started on the project.

I've gone eyeball-to-eyeball against the best naysayers in the world — people who have made a career of saying no. But when I prepare well and use these steps to promote my ideas, I bat around .900.

CHAPTER 15

What Have You Done Today?

The instructions to me were plain.

Fly from Portland, Oregon, to Chicago. Catch a commuter flight to Rhinelander, Wisconsin. (That's north of Green Bay.) Get my luggage and wait outside for a yellow school bus. Once the yellow school bus gets there, get inside. It would be a forty-minute ride to the motel. The next morning, I'd get in a pontoon boat at the motel and land at a boathouse across the lake.

That was the first part of the journey. The next part is what has had a profound effect on me to this day. You see, in 1986, I had signed up for a five-day seminar with Joe Sugarman. The cost of the seminar was a then-outrageous price $2,000, plus, of course, travel expenses and lodging.

Joe didn't invent ad writing, but he sure perfected it. His writing was Direct Response. You know, you'd read an ad about a product and feel compelled to immediately pick up the phone and buy the product right then and there. Joe made it easy for you to buy. He invented the

process of taking a credit card over the phone without a signature.

Through the years, I've used Joe's teachings many times. The ads in chapter 11 and chapter 12 were inspired by what I learned from Joe. If I forgot what he taught, no problem, I would just refer to his book *Advertising Secrets of the Written Word*. You can get it at Amazon.com.

I see Joe a couple of times a year, usually over in Maui, and I always marvel at his true marketing instincts.

Now, let's leap forward to July 27, 2009. These instructions were also plain.

Take a plane from Portland, Oregon, to Austin, Texas (with a transfer in Dallas). Get my luggage and go outside and grab a cab. In about forty minutes I'd be at the Wizard Academy. Since I'd arrive around 10 P.M., the place would be locked up. I was given a code to unlock the front gate. ("Relock it behind you.") Then I'd pull my suitcase down the hill to my lodging. ("The path to Engelbrecht House is steep, and difficult to navigate in the dark.")

This time, I was giving the seminar with the Wizard of Ads himself, Roy Williams. The seminar was "Make Big Things Happen Fast." It was two and half days with about fifty entrepreneurs on how to make big things happen quickly in a lousy economy.

I had known of Roy for about a decade. I learned about him from my *Marketing Outrageously* (and *Marketing Outrageously Redux*) publisher, Ray Bard. Ray had published Roy's book, *The Wizard of Ads*. I thought that book was every bit of genius as Joe Sugarman's book. Over the years, I meant to fly down to Austin just to have a beer or two with Roy and Ray. The years flew by without the beers. Then Ray put Roy and me together for the seminar at the Wizard Academy.

Wow! What an experience! Roy was, of course, terrific. Brilliant marketing mind. What pushed the experience even higher were the small business entrepreneurs that were electric and fun beyond anything I could have imagined.

While this chapter focuses on what you have done *today*, it's appropriate to take a step back and think about what single event you can do in the near future to crank up your creative juices. The thing I'm talking about isn't just going to a trade show or convention. I'm talking about going somewhere that *jolts* you, that whacks open your mind to the treasure trove of creativity that sometimes gets smothered. I've given you two examples of what I did. Find the right event for yourself. It will have as profound and lasting effect as anything else you do.

Asking the Toughest Question

This chapter starts with a little exercise.

Remember the favor I asked of you in the second chapter? You know, write down on a 3 × 5 card or paper napkin the question, "What's it gonna take to _____?"

Take that piece of paper out of your pocket. Place it nearby. In a little while I'm going to have you write something else on the other side. Once you do that, you'll be fully equipped to handle Marketing Outrageously.

A Hard Day's Night

As I drove home from work one dreary night a number of years ago in New Jersey, I couldn't imagine anyone more exhausted than I was after a twelve-hour day as president of the Nets. I had solved problems; I had resolved disputes. Just a typical day of meetings and decisions.

But as I drove, I asked myself one question: What did I do today to make money for the team?

I thought back on exactly what I had done that day.

- **I had spent about four hours working up a budget with several department heads.** That was important. If it's done right, budgeting can help marketers make a lot of money for the company in the coming year.

- **I had spent two hours with lawyers.** This wasn't a waste of time; we had legal issues to resolve. Resolving them wouldn't produce revenue, but it could save us a lot of trouble and money.

- **One hour had been devoted to architecture.** The Nets had been practicing in a gym built at a truck terminal — adequate, but not glamorous. You'd never mistake the locker room as something that would be featured in *Architectural Digest*. In the age of free agency in the NBA, I felt that we were getting into the recruiting business, and a fancy practice facility was one of the recruiting tools. I spent an hour with an architect discussing a possible new building.

- **One hour was spent reviewing some new direct-response ads** we would be running the following week.

- **Two hours went to phone calls.** I try to return all phone calls within twenty-four hours.

- **Two hours disappeared into lunch** and — I couldn't quite account for the rest.

Most of the things I had done were necessary. None of them had been a waste of time. If they had been, I would have delegated them. After all, isn't that the benefit of experience?

Nevertheless, if a prosecutor had put me on the witness stand under oath and asked me, "What did you do to directly make money for the Nets today?" I couldn't have given a direct answer. I might have said, "The meeting with the ad agency. The right direct response ad will lead to tens of thousands of dollars in new business."

"Today, Mr. Spoelstra. *Today,"* the prosecutor would insist. "What did you do to make money for the Nets *today?"*

As my attorney, you might jump up and say that the prosecutor was badgering the witness. You'd ask for a recess so we could somehow come up with a defense.

I'd say I was guilty as charged. You'd tell me I was being too hard on myself. As president, or even as marketing director, my function was to *lead,* not just *do* — to create an environment that would lead to increased revenue tomorrow, next month, next year. After all, the planning and strategizing I did months ago was making money for the team today.

I was innocent, you'd say. I could walk.

Except for one small item: you wouldn't have known about the vow I had made long ago.

The Vow

About fifteen years before you agreed to be my defense counsel, I was vice president of marketing for the Portland Trail Blazers. There were two people in that department: myself and an assistant. Our job was to increase our revenues from local sponsorships.

This we did. As we brought in more and more money, we added staff. Within a few years, marketing had twenty people, and I found myself doing more managing and less selling. Instead of making all the sales calls, as I had done at the beginning, I was making few or none.

On my way home from work one night, I asked myself, "What did you do today to make money for the Blazers?"

I came up with the same answer I did fifteen years later with the Nets.

That's when I made the vow.

My vow was this: No matter how my job and responsibilities grew, and no matter where my career took me, I would make at least one sales call a day.

I thought, How difficult can that be? Not that hard, I decided. After all, one sales call takes only an hour — for instance, one hour of not meeting with a lawyer.

I had some pretty good reasons for making that vow:

- **It reinforced why I was there.** As we had grown, I had been getting immersed in the responsibilities and intricacies of managing. But I was there to raise revenue, pure and simple, and that was how I was going to be measured. Making a sales call a day refocused me on my primary responsibility.

- **It reinforced to the staff how important increasing revenue was.** When the staff sees the president or marketing director or janitor out hustling for new business, it doesn't take them too long to figure out raising the revenue is an unwritten corporate mission statement.

- **It kept me in touch with the market.** Any good marketer can read all the product research available and *sound* knowledgeable, but keeping a personal *feel* for the market is essential. The best way to get the feel of the market is to make sales calls. Believe me, the people you are trying to sell to will tell you revealing things about your product.

- **It stimulated creativity.** When a prospect rips your company, you can say something nasty or you can get creative. A car is a good place to be alone and think: How can we reach this person? I've had some of my best ideas while riding in a car after we got mauled by a prospect.

- **It generated sales.** The fact is that you will bring in more sales. It impresses a prospect when a president or marketing director accompanies the salesperson. In fact, you'll find that with some salespeople you make a terrific team that is unstoppable. This happened when I was at the New Jersey Nets. I hired a guy named Brett Yormark for sponsorship sales. Brett had a tremendous work ethic and sales instinct. When he and I would go out on a sales call, it wasn't fair to the prospect. We'd play off each other like Joe Montana and Jerry Rice. We scored sale after sale after sale, even against the most difficult prospects. That hour and a half that I would spend with Brett — our leading salesperson — was valuable to the company. The time accelerated Brett's progress, making him even better. And for me it was really a lot of fun.

Whoa! That's Not My Job

Of course, you can sit down over a cup of coffee and come up with plenty of reasons why you, as president or marketing director, shouldn't make a sales call a day:

- **I don't have the time.** This sounds reasonable. But if God came down and whispered in your ear, "Find an hour and a half today to make a sales call, or you're going to hell,"

you'd find the time. If you work up a sweat and convince yourself that you clearly don't have time, buy a book on time management. We're talking *revenue* here; somehow you have to find the time.

- **My background is finance, not sales.** Yes, you're an expert at cutting costs. But what works best is cutting costs *and* raising revenues. If you don't feel comfortable about sales, the best way to become comfortable is to make sales calls. Who knows, you might become a terrific salesperson. Some of the best salespeople I know came out of the finance field. Even if you don't become a terrific salesperson, you will have sent the message to the troops how important raising revenue is by just making that one sales call a day.

- **We don't have local prospects to call on.** This one is a pretty good excuse. If a company's sales are national or even global, it's difficult to adhere to a one-sales-call-a-day policy. However, I won't let you off the hook that easily. Here are two ideas for you:

  - **Travel.** When you're traveling to branch offices, I assume there are customers there. That's right, one sales call a day while you're at a branch office. Maybe two sales calls a day or more. You would be sending the same message of how important revenues are to the company.

  - **Phone calls.** Accompanying a salesperson is just as important a reason as seeing a prospect. Once you do accompany a salesperson, keep his or her name on your Rolodex. Every once in a while, call that salesperson. Hear how things are going out in the field. Heck, in this situation, you could easily make two sales calls a day.

- **I don't like to make sales calls.** That's a wee bit understandable. After all, a sales call can cut the heart out of a day. And, alas, a meeting with a lawyer might have to be postponed. But let's go back to the original premise for being a marketing person: *to ramp up revenue.* It might be distasteful to some to make sales calls; however, using sales calls is one of the best tools I know of sending the message to employees and customers that you're serious about ramping up revenue.

A Call a Day, the Easy Way

The tough part of a sales call is not making the sale, it's everything that leads up to it – –making the appointment, juggling the schedule, preparing the material. I left that to the salesperson and did the easy stuff: go for a nice ride with the salesperson, spend

an hour or two talking about how great the company is, close the deal, give the salesperson a pat on the back, go back to the regular grind.

It didn't matter to me who the prospect was. What mattered was two things:

1. **The salesperson.** Salespeople knew that if they needed me to help close a sale, I'd be there. When there wasn't a big sale to help close, I would just rotate my calls among the salespeople, often leaving the decision until minutes before one of them was scheduled to leave for an appointment.

2. **The time frame.** We had twenty salespeople at the New Jersey Nets. If I could find a free hour in the afternoon

and hadn't already made arrangements, I checked to see who in the office had a sales appointment that would get me back within an hour or so, then invited myself along.

Aren't these actions really the sales manager's responsibility? Yes, the sales manager can, and should, do these things. Why? For the same reasons the company president or marketing director should do them:

- It reinforces why the sales manager is there — to raise revenues.

- It tells the staff how important increasing revenue is.

- It keeps the sales manager in touch with the market.

- It stimulates the creation of new revenue ideas.

- It generates sales.

If you're trying to ramp up revenues, all these reasons work for the sales manager as well as for you. You could add another reason, like training, but that's a different book.

What to Write on the Other Side

What's it gonna take to be the best department in our company?

What did I do today to make money for my company?

At the beginning of this chapter, I asked you to take out of your pocket the piece of paper on which you had written, "What's it gonna take . . . ?" because I was going to ask you to write something on the back of it. Here's what I want you to write. It's another question:

What did I do today to make money for my company?

Go ahead, write that down on the other side of the paper. I'll wait.

That piece of paper is going to become an important tool for you. Just two simple questions. They could have a lot of different answers. But to really get into Marketing Outrageously, you've got to ask yourself those two questions — every day.

When You and I Meet

Someday, somewhere, you and I may meet. It could be anywhere — on an airplane, at a conference, on adjoining barstools overlooking a Maui beach. After we introduce ourselves, I'll ask you one thing:

"Let me see the card in your pocket. You know, the one with 'What's it gonna take?' written on one side and 'What did I do today to make money for my company?' on the other." If you're carrying it, you're probably doing really well.

And even though you are doing really well, I'll buy the drinks.

A SIMPLE TEST YOU CAN TAKE

1. Which would your staff want you to do most?
   a. Give a twenty-minute speech to them every day.
   b. Make one sales call per day with your company's sales staff.

    c. Run the marketing from your ivory tower by reading research.

2. You think I'm pretty severe in asking you to make a sales call a day. It would be more reasonable to make one a month or one a year. (True/False)

3. You do things for the company that are more important than the revenue that one sales call a day could bring in. (True/False)

Answers

1. b. I think your staff would want you to make the one-sales-call-a-day choice. Calling a full staff meeting every day to give a speech would get pretty tedious. A basketball team naturally gets together daily to practice. But if you're willing to spend an hour a day, every day, preparing your speech, and if you can keep it interesting and not repeat yourself, go for it. You might become a motivational speaker and get $50,000 per speech. Let's see, fifty grand a day, five days a week, fifty weeks a year — that's $12 million and change. Hmmm.

2. False. If you're in a position that has an effect on raising revenue, then you have to take sales calls seriously. Sure, there are times when you're forced to slack off a bit. If you're really up to your eyeballs in some marketing project, it makes sense to drop back to three sales calls for the week, or even two. But don't get in the habit of interpreting everything as a "special circumstance."

Raising revenue is not easy or automatic. It takes constant and consistent effort in the field. If you aren't doing one sales call a day right now, try it for a month. Then evaluate it. You'll find that you're more in touch with the marketplace than ever before, and you'll gain a feel for its inner workings that a safecracker would be envious of.

3. False. Yes, you probably do more important things than bringing in one sales call's worth of revenue per day. So why isn't the answer true? Because the other reasons for making one sales call a day are far more important:

- It reinforces why you're at the company — that's right, to raise revenues.

- It tells your staff how important increasing revenue is.

- It keeps you in touch with the market.

- It stimulates the creation of new ideas for raising revenue.

- It generates sales.

Yes, you do very important things, but none are more important than raising revenue. One sales call a day will remind you of that, day after day after day.

CHAPTER 16

Employees to Kill For

Years ago, my wife asked me to fix a dripping faucet in our home. "I'll take care of it Saturday morning," I said.

On the fateful morning, I got my toolbox out of the garage. In it there was a hammer, a few screwdrivers, some masking tape, and a chisel. Clearly I didn't have the tools to fix a dripping faucet, unless I could pound on it with the hammer until the dripping stopped.

A trip to the hardware store added a pipe wrench and a handful of other wrenches to the toolbox. I also bought an assortment of washers — those little round things that somehow stop a faucet from dripping.

Two hours later I had replaced the washers and tightened everything back up. My knuckles were bloody, but the job was done. I called my wife in to see the wonderful non-dripping faucet. As she stood reverently in front of the sink, I turned on the water, then turned it off.

Drip, drip, drip.

That's when I made one of the more important decisions in my life. I vowed that I would do only the things I was good at, and that I would not do things I wasn't good at.

I explained this revelation to my wife. "I figure if I only do things I'm good at, and don't waste time doing what I'm not good at, I'll do better at what I do well. If I do better at what I do well, I'll get paid more, and we can afford to hire people to do what they do well."

I suggested that from that time forward, when something needed fixing around the house, she should call some professional to fix it.

"Even a washer on a faucet?" she asked. "Plumbers charge $35 an hour."

"Yes, even a washer," I said. "That's a lot to fix a dripping faucet, but it will actually get fixed, and I won't get frustrated trying to do something I'm not good at and never will be good at. Besides, it's good for the economy. We'll be keeping a specialist employed."

She looked at me. She looked at my knuckles. She started to laugh. Then she said, like one of the world's great diplomats, "It's worth a try."

Since then, I've always spent at least four hours on the weekend doing what I do well. Maybe I do nothing but read a marketing book, but for me that's a lot more productive than fixing a faucet or mowing the lawn. Over the years, we've gladly paid plumbers, electricians, painters, and gardeners to do what they do best. I'm convinced it has paid off in higher earnings for me.

I've tried to follow a similar philosophy in business: do the things I'm good at, delegate the rest. What I'm good at is marketing and sales. Sure, I've acquired pieces of other skills — budgeting, management, even legal issues — but what I do best is marketing and sales.

Think about it, though: How often do you get sidetracked trying to do something you're not good at?

So, when I get sidetracked now, I think of my bloodied knuckles and the time I pretended to be a weekend plumber. Then I get back to what I do well.

Valuing Your Experts

"Who are the most important people to our company? The shareholders, of course."

You hear this all the time. The CEO of a public company says it on *Wall Street Week in Review* or in a *Wall Street Journal* interview.

The CEO adds, "Next in importance are our customers."

Nobody mentions employees.

For companies like these, here's the order of importance, apparently:

1. Shareholders
2. Customers
3. Employees

I believe this is ass-backwards. I prefer the ranking you'll find in any good Marketing Outrageously company:

1. Employees
2. Customers
3. Shareholders

What does this mean? Double everybody's pay? Reduce the forty-hour work week to twenty? Turn Casual Friday into Sloppy All Week Long?

Of course not.

What would life be like with this outrageous concept of placing employees first on the priority list — ahead of customers and shareholders?

Here's what:

If you
- treat your employees fairly . . .
- inspire them . . .
- let them try outrageous things without fear of getting fired or humiliated in front of their peers . . .

Employees will
- work harder, because they want to . . .
- work smarter, because they are allowed to . . .
- think up outrageous ideas that bring outrageously positive results . . .
- care for their customers as they would a rich, dying aunt who is still revising her will . . .
- not leave the company — not even the most talented employees — because they are having too much fun.

Customers will
- love your company, because it has such happy employees . . .
- buy more . . .
- tell their friends about this outrageous company and its friendly, happy people . . .
- bring in new customers, who will buy even more.

Shareholders will
- like all this new buying and the resulting surge in revenue . . .
- like the way the employees figured out how to do things better, thus making each product cost less to produce . . .
- love the higher profits that come from higher revenues and lower costs . . .
- enjoy watching stock values rise . . .
- marvel at dividends that are bigger than ever . . .
- be happy as hell and brag about what a great investment they made.

Where the Employee Is King

"We already treat our employees well," a CEO will tell you. "They're paid better than the industry average, we've got a great health plan, and there's free parking. What else could an employee want?"

Good pay and health insurance and free parking are all things that a company *should* provide. Employees expect it. But what will *really* catch employees' attention? Something not every company does — something outrageous: *show* them that employees are the company's *number-one priority.*

Here's how we did it with the New Jersey Nets:

1. **Employee comic handbook.** Most employee handbooks read like a summons — probably because they were written by lawyers. Companies often use these handbooks to cover their legal ass. At the Nets, we made the employees' handbook fun and friendly. We covered the essentials, but we made it easy to read and used cartoons to entertain and to illustrate the main points.

2. **Free education.** Many companies offer to help employees continue their education in work-related subjects, usually by paying half or more of the tuition. We took this a step further — right into the outrageous.

Employees of the Nets could take a course in *any* subject whatsoever. If you wanted to take gardening lessons, we'd pay for it. Golf lessons? We'll pay for it. Skydiving? It's on us. Computer programming? Go for it. You name it, you do it, we pay for it — 100 percent of it.

Why would we do such an outrageously generous and goofy thing? Couldn't we go broke paying for it? You'd think so, but it didn't work out that way. Even with no limits, few employees signed up. We spent less than $100 per employee on average.

Any company could afford a lot more, and should encourage employees to take classes, whether in metallurgy, accounting, or astrophysics. Those who do will become better people for it. They'll tell their fellow employees about the fun they're having in their gardening class. They'll walk faster, feel better, be more energized. Even employees who don't take you up on the offer will appreciate knowing they have the option. And if they finally enroll in a class, they will walk a little brisker, feel a little more energized.

3. **No-miss policy.** I've always been surrounded by people with a great work ethic. That's good. What's bad, though, is that these people miss a lot of important family events. Have you ever heard these lines (or said them yourself)?

- "My son is pitching today in Little League, but I have to work — this project is too important to miss."

- "My daughter's in the school play, but we're working like crazy to finish this project."

- "Today's my wife's birthday, and they're having a surprise lunch for her, but my client is in town and we've got to get approvals, and . . ."

At the Nets, you couldn't miss family events and celebrations because of work. The rule was, you were not allowed to let work cause you to miss those functions. You might want to miss them for reasons of your own, but you couldn't use work as an excuse.

When I tell others about this policy, their first question is usually "Didn't people abuse the privilege?"

"No," I answer. "In fact, they didn't go to enough events."

We wanted people to go to as many as possible. Why? Because when parents take the time to see their kids doing something special, it creates fond memories for the whole family. The kid remembers that Mom and Dad were there when he won that spelling bee or when she kicked the winning goal. The parents have irreplaceable memories of watching their kids grow up.

When a parent takes two hours out of the middle of a workday to watch a kid in a school play, it's not as if the company's being shorted. The employee will easily make up that time and will work smarter. Can a spelling bee benefit the employee's family, the employee, and the company? Yes, it can.

4. **Forced vacations.** When I started with the Nets, I was told about the Vacation Bank. If you earned two weeks' vacation time in a year and didn't use it, it went into your Vacation Bank.

"What's this bank good for?" I asked. "If you didn't take a vacation for five years, could you use all of that time — let's say ten weeks — for one vacation?"

"Of course not. The Vacation Bank is for when you leave the Nets. You get more separation pay."

"How does separation pay fit in?" I asked.

"Well, let's say you've been here for ten years, and because you're an executive, you get more vacation time. Let's say you get four weeks per year. If you haven't taken a vacation in ten years, you have forty weeks of pay coming to you when you leave the company. That's the Vacation Bank. If you were fired, you'd of course get more because you'd get severance pay."

I thought, If I didn't take a vacation in ten years, I'd be less effective each year. I'd find it harder each year to come up with outrageous ideas, and a lot harder to encourage or even tolerate outrageous ideas from others. I'd probably get pretty weary. I'd have less energy. There wouldn't be any tread left on these tires. Then I would either quit or get fired. But not to worry, I'd have forty weeks in the Vacation Bank.

We closed the Vacation Bank.

We eliminated the class dispar-ity in vacation accumulation. No longer could executives take longer vacations than non-executives. We based vaca-tion time on length of service.

We made taking a vaca-tion mandatory. You could *not* spend your vacation time at work. And while you were on vacation, you couldn't phone in. Not even once.

We were selfish about this. Yes, we wanted you to enjoy your vacation, but most of all we wanted you to recharge yourself for the challenge of marketing the New Jersey Nets for another year.

(There were a few longtime employees who had over fifty days in the Vacation Bank. Instead of zeroing out their accounts, we let them draw an additional five days a year to stretch their normal vacation time. But if they didn't use it, they'd lose it.)

5. **Six-week paid sabbatical.** After working three years for the Nets, you could take a six-week sabbatical. There were strings, however. To qualify, you had to propose to do something a little more than interesting. For example, if one of our young salespeople wanted to go to the beach and drink beer and ogle girls for six weeks, that might be interesting, but it wouldn't qualify. But if he wanted to go to the Jersey Shore and help build a house — and drink beer and ogle girls in his spare time — then that would be inter-esting and constructive.

Yes, the guidelines were loose. Our staff understood this. But as early as year two of this policy, here's the kind of conversations we were hearing:

"I want to work for a pro basketball team in Spain," said one young salesperson who was already taking Spanish lessons on our free education program.

"I want to work for the Major League Baseball head office," said another.

"I want to sail from Los Angeles to Honolulu . . ."

All the "wants" I heard were in some way educational. That's exactly what we had intended. If a two-week vacation could recharge a person's batteries, we hoped a six-week sabbatical would install a whole new set of more powerful batteries.

6. **Help in negotiating your next job.** We hired a lot of young people, and because our basketball team was so dismal, we needed them to learn much faster than normal. So we trained them thoroughly, and kept on training them week after week after week. To accelerate their managerial experience, we made sales team captains of some who had sold tickets for two years or more. This was more Big Brother than Big Boss, but it gave 24- and 25-year-olds some limited management experience which would enhance their career options.

Other teams that had trouble selling tickets began to take notice of our success. We knew they would try to pick off some of our most talented people — and we encouraged it.

How in the world could we encourage our best and brightest to leave us? Now, that was truly outrageous and stupid!

Here's the reasoning, as I explained it to our young staffers:

"Because a lot of you are quickly developing valuable skills, other teams will want to steal you away. That's okay. We don't want to lose you, but we know each of you has your own career. If you can take a giant step along your career path with another team, we'll help you.

"When another team approaches you, let us know. If it's something you want to do, we'll help you negotiate the best deal. We don't want to lose you, but if we have to, we don't want it to be for a piddling amount of money. We want you to get a lot more money and a lot more responsibility when you leave."

We did help negotiate some deals. We hated to lose budding superstars, but if we lost them to a great money or career opportunity, we were living our commitment: that everybody has a career, and working for the Nets should enhance that career. That's a terrific message for staffers who stayed with us, and for new recruits: If you learn our marketing system, you can make it big with the Nets, or you can make it big with another team.

The reality is, we would have lost some of our best and brightest anyway. By helping them get a better deal, we used that loss to demonstrate our commitment to the other staffers.

Equally important, we were able to help them avoid "career killers." One of our most talented people turned down an attractive offer because the team owner didn't want any of that Marketing Outrageously stuff. He wanted to do everything through publicity. In two years, that owner ended up hiring and firing three different ticket sales managers. Not one of them came from the Nets.

Some of these employee policies may seem a bit outrageous. They certainly go against the grain of what many of us have been taught. But let's look back to our premise. The most important entities in a Marketing Outrageously company are, in order of importance:

1. Employees
2. Customers
3. Shareholders

If the employees have energy, if they are *passionate* about their jobs, if they keep learning all the time — including their own time — then they will be better employees. They will be far more conscious of a customer's needs; they will get more customers with their energy and passion and knowledge; they will keep more customers coming back. Revenues will rise. Profits will rise. Shareholders will smile, and laugh, and thank their lucky stars that they hold stock in this fine company.

A SIMPLE TEST YOU CAN TAKE

1. Won't you lose some of your most valued employees after they take the six-week paid sabbatical?
   a. No.
   b. Maybe.
   c. Yes, but that's okay.

2. Won't some people abuse the privilege of free education?
   a. No.
   b. Maybe.
   c. Yes, but that's okay.

3. Can we afford to let our employees miss that much work time through vacations or sabbaticals?
   a. No.
   b. Maybe.
   c. Yes.

Answers

1. c. Yes, you will lose some. Suppose an employee uses the six weeks to build houses for poor people in Thailand, then wants to build more, and so resigns. That's okay — even if the employee is a very valuable employee. Remember, each employee has his or her own career. If you respect that, the employees who don't run off to build houses in Thailand will be better employees. Companies lose valuable employees all the time. My feeling is that a sabbatical refreshes and brings back employees who would otherwise have grown stale and moved on.

2. c. Yes, some people will take course after course after course. That's okay. I think it makes them more interesting people and more productive employees. If they didn't take courses, they might be doing something not as interesting, like watching TV all night or hanging around in bars.

We did have some limitations at the Nets. If you were trying to get an advanced degree, that was terrific, but we would pay for only six credit hours per semester. Although we wanted you to take advantage of the free education, we didn't want you to become a full-time student at our expense.

We also set boundaries on cost. If you wanted to take a university course, it had to be at a public university, where the costs are much lower. If your course wasn't available at a public university, we would pay what the course would have cost if it had been.

There was no limit on subject matter — it just had to be some kind of formal course. A private course in owl stuffing? Yeah, we'd pay for that.

3. b. Maybe. If you have a company with only two or three employees, it might be hard to allow one a six-week paid sabbatical. But if you could hire temporary help or automate, it might work out. What would you do if that employee got run over by a bus and couldn't come to work for six weeks?

Suppose, however, you have a lot of employees. Then it should certainly be possible. If anybody is so critical to your operation that you can't allow her a sabbatical, then you have a potential disaster on your hands. What if she quits? What if that bus comes back?

Each company should, like a pro sports team, develop its own "bench strength." This bench should be able to take over the operation, think on its own, and implement what it has learned about running the company.

When I was at the Portland Trail Blazers, I began taking three-week vacations to Hawaii. My instructions to the staff were simple: "I'll be gone for three weeks. I'm not leaving a phone number where I can be reached. You will not be able to track me down. You are free, and obligated, to make all decisions. If you want to change things, change them."

"What if your house burns down?" one of the employees asked. "Wouldn't you want to know?"

"Well, if my house burns down, there's not much I can do about it in Hawaii except ruin my vacation. So don't even try to track me down and tell me. Soon I'll be back. I'll see right away that my house has burned down. I'll check into a hotel, come to work, and call my insurance company."

CHAPTER 17

Outrageous Mosaic

Magician David Copperfield can make an elephant disappear, in full view of the audience and the television cameras. Pretty neat illusion, eh?

That's child's play, I say.

Name a magician who can make millions of jobs disappear. Remember a character named "Chainsaw Al" Dunlap? He was a CEO in the 1990s who could lop off 50,000 jobs in a heartbeat. (Pity that many other CEOs have used him as a role model instead of focusing on cranking up the revenue.)

Millions upon millions of jobs have disappeared over the last century. If this were 1910 and I asked you to name a job that would almost disappear before 2010, would you have said, "Farmer"?

At the dawn of the twentieth century, about 80 percent of the jobs in the United States were in, or connected with, agriculture. A hundred years later that figure is down to about 3 percent. An entire industry, nearly gone! Where did it go?

It didn't go — it evolved. When Henry Ford came up with the assembly line, it didn't take long for the United States to turn itself into a manufacturing powerhouse. When we figured out how to make the same product cheaper in another country, we evolved into a service economy. Then we transformed ourselves into a world-leading computers-and-software economy.

There have been several constants over the past hundred years. One is that the United States still leads the world in producing food. That is true in part because America has a lion's share of the world's most fertile farmland. But it's also true that our agricultural productivity is second to none, thanks to lessons Henry Ford and others taught us.

Another twentieth-century constant: we are the best marketers in the world. We've been better marketers ever since Sears-Roebuck invented the product catalog that gave farmers ready access to everything from cotton dresses to combines. Today we send out millions of catalogs without even printing or mailing them. Ahh, the Internet.

Now that you're reading this in the twenty-first century, you can ask me the same question I would have asked you in the year 1910: "Which job category will disappear in the twenty-first century?"

Before I can speak, you answer it yourself: "Stockbrokers."

I nod in agreement. The Internet will surely make stockbrokers the blacksmiths of the twenty-first century.

Then I say, "I'd like to add something to the list."

You wait.

I say, "Retail as we know it."

Now, don't dash to your PC and sell off your retail stocks. Just as farming survived and prospered (who would ever have thought we could easily feed 300 million people in our own country and countless millions more around the globe?), retail will certainly survive and prosper. It will just be different — a lot different.

Internet business is, of course, another form of retail. Will it replace bricks-and-mortar retail? I don't think so, but the Internet will dramatically change it. What will happen to the big shopping malls? They may survive, or they may become big distribution areas, or schools, or prisons — who can say? The retailers who survive and prosper will be those who best combine e-business with bricks and mortar.

My candidate for the pioneer of New Retail is someone you probably haven't heard of. It's not Microsoft's Bill Gates nor Amazon.com's Jeff Bezos. The pioneer I have in mind is Steve Wynn.

Who's Steve Wynn? Well, above all, he's a marketer. He's the guy who invented Las Vegas as we know it. His casinos have distinctive, elaborate themes, much like the false fronts on a movie set. Inside, the casinos all look alike — the same slot machines, video poker, crap tables, blackjack games. It's the  "movie fronts" that draw people into this casino as opposed to that casino, where they dutifully lose their money while enjoying being part of the big show.

Is this what Big Retail is destined to look like — Big Entertainment? After all, if we wanted the lowest price, we'd just order through the Internet, wouldn't we? We'll see some amazing changes in the twenty-first century. Technology will bring us a never-ending stream of products we couldn't have dreamed of just five years before. But when all is said and done, somebody will have to get somebody else to buy some other person's product. That's marketing.

Just as King Gillette prospered at the beginning of the last century, marketers will flourish throughout the twenty-first. And those who do flourish won't be by-the-textbook marketers — they'll be outrageous marketers.

So when you have a marketing challenge, block out some time, go into your office, close the door, check for hidden cameras — and push the outrageous envelope.

This Bass-Ackwards Book

A friend of mine in Japan always reads the last chapter of a book first. "Saves time," says Yokoi. I'll assume for a moment that you've done just that.

Since this is the first chapter you have read, I'll use it to give you a mental mosaic of the book. Here are the essential parts:

- **Never use bland marketing.** If you have a lot more dollars than your competition, you probably think **you** can get away with bland. Maybe you can — for a while. But you'd better build an altar in your bedroom and make perpetual novenas that none of your competitors use outrageous marketing. If they do, they can hurt you really bad. So, even if you're bloated with marketing dollars, you should be Marketing Outrageously.

- **In every marketing project, think outrageous.** Do you remember those paint-by-number kits? Do you sometimes find yourself using a similar process in your marketing? Sometimes it just seems easier to put yellow in all the spaces numbered eight and red in spaces numbered two, then hang it on your wall and gaze at what you have wrought. Although painting by the numbers might be a diversion, like doing a crossword puzzle, you'll never see the result hanging in an art gallery. Nor will you see a formula-driven marketing project stir the hearts of your customers.

- **At the New Jersey Nets, we did everything with an eye for the outrageous.** Even something as mundane as a ticket got special attention. Your season tickets came in a wooden cigar box with our logo burned into the top. Inside, along with the tickets, we included an "Owner's Manual" with all kinds of useful information — for instance, how to get our help jump-starting your dead battery after the game. We got a computer artist to design a different ticket for each of our forty-one home games, featuring one of our own players or even an opposing player. "Why go to all that trouble?" other teams would ask. "It's just tickets." But our philosophy was that we were in the entertainment business, starting the moment our fans received their tickets.

- **Expect tangible results from your advertising.** You can think image and identity, but think harder about building an image *and* selling your product at the same time. Look for The Ratio — how much money did you get for every dollar you spent?

- **Toss out Reach and Frequency; go for dominance.** You might consider this truly outrageous thinking. After all, we've been trained as marketers to reach as many people as we can, with at least a modicum of frequency. Well, a modicum of frequency never persuaded anybody to buy a product. Even if you reach fewer people, you can raise an army of customers if you reach them with frightening frequency.

- **Think the outrageous thought that you and your marketing can be the best.** Was there a little rah-rah in this book? Certainly. Bland marketing doesn't need cheerleaders, but doing the outrageous means taking a few risks — and I'm here to cheer you on.

In truth, the biggest risk in Marketing Outrageously isn't with customers. The biggest risk is in your own company, where "different" is often interpreted as "dangerous." Just remember: Doing something different, something outrageous, is a key step in making your marketing the best in your industry.

Help Is on the Way

Sometimes you may get a little tired of having to retreat to your office, shut the door, and check for hidden cameras in order to push the outrageous envelope. If so, here are a few places where you can get some help:

1. **Your ad agency.** Caution: Outrageous help doesn't come easy from your ad agency. You see, they've been carefully trained to mirror what you want. Their number-one job is like that of a United States senator — to be reelected, or in this case, retained. So you'll have to give your agency an outrageous assignment: Come up with a marketing strategy they are sure you will turn down. That's right, a marketing idea so outrageous that you will surely reject it outright. Now, prepare yourself to be disappointed.

Their first outrageous idea won't be very outrageous or different at all. Look on them with compassion; they have to crawl before they can walk. Give them another chance.

If they're any good at all, within two or three attempts they'll come up with something really outrageous — something that they *know* you won't approve. It will be great. Now all you have to do is have the guts to run with it.

2. **A marketing consultant.** I'm not recommending that you hire a marketing consulting firm to suggest new techniques in marketing — although that would be a good idea. I've got a better, more outrageous — even strange — idea for you: hire a marketing consulting firm to find ways of beating you.

Yes, that's right. To beat you. Here's how it works.

It works best if you hire the consultants anonymously. Your ad agency can probably do this (an outrageous idea!). The consultants' sole objective is to figure out ways of legitimately beating your company. They'll come up with some pretty good ideas. Some of these you can incorporate into whatever you're now doing. Others will uncover weaknesses in your organization that you weren't aware of. Now you can eliminate that Achilles' heel before it brings you tumbling down.

An alternative way — although not as effective — is to create a secret "maverick" group within your own company. The group's mission is to stay up nights thinking of ways to beat you. They write a marketing plan to accomplish that. Like the marketing consulting firm, this group will think up ideas you can latch onto right away, and others, more sinister, that you can prepare to protect yourself from.

This may sound like a weird idea, even beyond outrageous, but it will produce outrageously positive results for you.

3. **Attend at least one session of the Wizard Academy.** Go to the website, www.wizardacademy.org, to see the courses offered. The courses are two- to three-day affairs that will help you for years. When you look over the various courses, you will find at least three that you would be highly

interested in taking. Take one. You'll learn like crazy, but the best part is your classmates. They're like you, entrepreneurs with fire in the belly. The Wizard Academy is in Austin, Texas. Go there, experience it, and then go again.

4. **Extra-credit reading.** By the time I had children in school, paper routes had become big business — too big for a kid and a bike. So my kids had to make money an outrageous way: by reading. Who paid them? I did. Read five articles in *Time*, earn fifty cents. Ayn Rand's *Atlas Shrugged?* Twenty bucks. After all, *Atlas Shrugged* is over 1,000 pages!

Sorry, but you don't qualify for my compensation for reading. You read for the sheer pleasure of learning, or for extra credit on the quizzes at the end of each chapter. If you liked some of the thoughts in *Marketing Outrageously Redux,* here's more. You get extra credit for reading each of these marketers.

- **Joe Sugarman.** I think Joe invented ad writing, he's so good. He's widely considered one of the all-time greatest direct-response ad writers, but don't be fooled — he is perhaps the best outrageous marketer of all time. Joe's written four books: *Triggers, Advertising Secrets of the Written Word, Marketing Secrets of a Mail Order Maverick,* and *Television Secrets for Marketing Success.* Buy all four and immerse yourself in outrageous marketing.

- **Roy Williams.** Yep, Roy is the founder of the Wizard Academy, but I first ran across him by reading his first book, *The Wizard of Ads.* Look him up on Amazon and work your way through each one of his books.

- **Tom Peters.** You may wonder why I've included Tom here. After all, he's considered a management guru. That he is, but first and foremost, Tom's an outrageous thinker. I love his stuff. His ideas will give

you a big boost toward becoming an outrageous
marketer.

- **Al Ries.** If there's any book I wish I had written, it is
Ries's *22 Immutable Laws of Marketing,* the bible for
marketing. I've read it several times. I've listened to
the audio while on my treadmill at least as many
times. Once you've read *Laws,* you've got to read
Focus — then read it again. And again.

- **Roy Williams every week, fifty-two weeks a year.** I've
mentioned Roy's book *The Wizard of Ads* as one you
must read. But, if you're like me, you'd like to hear
from Roy every week. Well, he sends out a FREE
weekly e-letter, *The Monday Morning Memo.* Here's
the Internet address: www.mondaymorningmemo.
com. Each week, Roy gets me to *think* whether I want
to or not. Most of all, I look for him to *surprise me.*
Here's how to find the surprise. Double-click on the
main photo of the home page. Be forewarned: This is
like Alice falling through the rabbit hole. Once you
double-click on the main photo, a secret page will
pop up. Read it. Muse over it. Try *not* to think. You
can't. Marvelous! Then double-click on the photo on
that page. Keep doing it. Keep thinking. I'm amazed
how Roy gets me to think every week! It's free. So join
me in falling down the rabbit hole.

BONUS QUESTIONS

Thought you were through taking quizzes, didn't you? Well,
if you've maintained a perfect score up to now, you don't
need to take this final exam. You're already a terrifically outrageous marketer. But for the rest of you, here's a chance for
some bonus points.

1. I have indeed written, "What's it gonna take . . . ?" on one side of a piece of paper and "What did I do today to make money for my company?" on the other side. (True/False)

2. I'm going to think outrageously on every marketing project I'm involved in. (True/False)

Answers

1. True. Am I nagging? Yes, I am. Having that little card in your pocket is the best way I know to keep focused and centered on making Marketing Outrageously work for you, day after day, week after week, year after year.

2. True. This may seem a little outrageous by itself, and it probably is. But when I'm consulting, I see too many people just going through the motions, checking items on a to-do list. At the end of the week or month, all they've got is check marks. These check marks represent things that are done, but they are done blandly, with no impact.

I'm not against using checklists. In fact, I recommend that you use one. But in my system, you can write a check mark only next to items where you thought outrageously and applied your outrageous thinking to the project. If you thought bland, no check mark.

At the end of the day or week, you wouldn't want to look at your list and see no check marks, would you? So, c'mon, start now, start thinking outrageously now, start Marketing Outrageously now.

Since you've read this far, I'll give you the first check mark. It's up to you to fill in the rest.

Outrageously done?	**Action**
☑	Read *Marketing Outrageously Redux*
☐	Written "What's it gonna take?" card
	Your next marketing function:
☐	_____
☐	_____
☐	_____

This book has been great fun to write. Even so, it's more fun to market outrageously. Try it; you'll like it. Then tell me about how some outrageous marketing worked for you. Give me all the fun details. If you do, the next book might be coauthored by you and me and hundreds of others.

Have fun, market outrageously, ramp up revenue stunningly, and make lots of money.

Dedication

Tthere's one person, more than any other, to whom I dedicate this book — and I think you know that person on a first-name basis.

At first, I was thinking of another outrageous marketer, Steve Pettise. Steve is a longtime friend and a guy who increased the same-store sales at a national restaurant chain for over 100 straight months. Now, that is really outrageous. But Steve already knows how good he is without my dedicating this book to him.

I thought of my family, of course. My wife of over forty years, Lisa, certainly deserves the dedication for all the cheering she has had to do. My daughter, Monica, is an outrageous marketer in her own right. Son Erik is the head coach with the Miami Heat and, with team president Pat Riley, is really outrageous in the unbridled dedication to winning. So I dedicate this book to them, but they do take a secondary position. I think, however, they'll applaud the top person this book is dedicated to.

Then there's Ray Bard, my publisher. Every writer should have Ray and his people as his or her publisher, but he's not the top dog in this dedication.

I think of the people that have had an important influence on me over the years. Two of them, Joe Sugarman and Roy Williams, are the greatest marketers ever. Joe is a genius of the written word; Roy is a genius of the spoken word. I've done seminars with Roy at his Wizard Academy in Austin, Texas, and it's a blast of thinking. Both have books, and each of their books should be read, underlined, and kept in a special place.

Then there are the Mandalay folks. I'll start with Peter Guber; I think the phrase "thinking outside the box" was invented for him. Then Howie Nuchow. Howie was one of my young warriors at the New Jersey Nets, and then I worked with him for ten years at Mandalay Baseball Properties. It was so much fun working with Howie. He is now president of CAA (Creative Artists Agency), the monster talent agency in entertainment and sports. Bob Murphy is another. Bob is the president of the Dayton Dragons; he's a great detail guy who has become a great outrageous marketer. Steve Delay was another one of my young warriors at the N.J. Nets and is now Exec VP at Mandalay.

My mind runs to the great marketers I've known. Some are already mentioned in this book — like Larry Weinberg, the owner of the Portland Trail Blazers from the '70s to the late '80s. He loved outrageous ideas! What a godsend to me. Others, like David Stern, the commissioner of the NBA, deserves mention for all the help he has provided me over the years. David is lawyer-trained, but he might be the best marketer in the world. Gary Bettman, commissioner of the NHL, is also lawyer-trained, but he is in the elite class of marketers.

When I run through all these names, there's one name that keeps on jumping to the top. But first, let me ask you to do one more writing assignment. This one is easy. Just print your name on the line below.

I dedicate this book to _____.
After all, you've taken the time to read to this very last page. To me this means that you're entertaining the concept of Marketing Outrageously. That's important. The world needs more outrageous marketers. So, above all those talented people mentioned above, I dedicate this book to you. I cheer you on.

Index